1. A Basket of Bread

A BASKET OF BREAD

A BOOK OF MEDITATIONS

A Basket of Bread

An Anthology of Selected Poems

Love: a basket of bread
from which to eat
for years to come;
good loaves, fragrant and warm,
miraculously multiplied:
the basket never empty.
the bread never stale.

CATHERINE DE VINCK

ALBA·HOUSE **alba house** N E W · Y O R K

SOCIETY OF ST. PAUL, 2187 VICTORY BLVD., STATEN ISLAND, NEW YORK 10314

ST PAULS

Library of Congress Cataloging-in-Publication Data

de Vinck, Catherine.
    A basket of bread: an anthology of selected poems / Catherine de
Vinck.
        p.   cm.
    ISBN 0-8189-0769-X
    1. Christian poetry, American.   I. Title.   II. Title: Book of
meditations.
PS3554.E928B37   1996
811'.54 — dc20   96-34565
                                                    CIP

Produced and designed in the United States of America by the
Fathers and Brothers of the Society of St. Paul,
2187 Victory Boulevard, Staten Island, New York 10314,
as part of their communications apostolate.

ISBN: 0-8189-0769-X

Printing Information:

Current Printing - first digit	1	2	3	4	5	6	7	8	9	10

Year of Current Printing - first year shown

1996	1997	1998	1999	2000	2001	2002	2003	2004	2005

To Archbishop Joseph Raya
with love and gratitude

Table of Contents

From: *Through the Gateless Gate*

Introduction

Catherine de Vinck is not only a dear friend, she is also my favorite poet. If I praise her work too highly you would surely be justified in suspecting that I am biased, but there are many others who see something quite rare in her poetic gift.

Thomas Merton wrote to Catherine back in 1966, "you have a wonderful Blake-like response to the sacred world."

Cornelia Jessey Sussman expressed these sentiments: "...perhaps there are only three or four every century... given the gift to voice the eternal vision, to put into words what we know cannot be put into words. Like the sun breaking through the clouds of a dark frozen winter sky, such poets bring the good news that winter is not forever."

Sally Cuneen writing in "The Critic" had this comment: "Catherine de Vinck is an extraordinary poet, sensual, evocative, deeply religious. She found time not to promote her reputation, but simply to write her poems which spring from a genuine love of simple realities like food, weather and people, and suggest a discipline that had turned them and suffering into a poetry of joy."

Poetry is more than language, it transcends what it signifies and enables us to see beyond the existing order. The poet is the primary mediator between God and creature, teaching us that truth cannot be reduced to abstract reason or philosophical formulas.

God is not of this world, though He dwells in it. He belongs more to the order of poetry. We can only speak of our

Maker in images that transcend the present moment. We feel there is something beyond all that we see, something we can never conceive or imagine. I have found Catherine's poetry a satisfying form of spiritual reading which leads me gently to the prayer of contemplation.

In order to love God one needs to know Him, the imagination needs freedom to soar beyond our mental limits. The poet invites us to explore another level of reality. The symbolic language of poetry is itself a prayer which transports us to the world of mystery.

Who is this woman Catherine de Vinck, and how did she become such a gifted poet?

Born in Brussels, Catherine spoke French and Flemish as a child. She lived through the Nazi occupation of Belgium, and after World War II married Baron Jose de Vinck. She didn't learn English until they came to the United States in 1948. Since then three American universities have awarded her honorary doctorates for her literary accomplishments.

Her second child, Oliver was a beautiful baby but it soon became obvious that he was blind, mute, brain damaged and destined to remain an infant until his death at the age of 33. His mother's love made Oliver's life a sweet mystery instead of a tragic nightmare. The following excerpt from a 1977 article she was asked to write for "Sign" magazine in 1977 may give you some sense of the woman behind the poetry.

> For many years I was confined to the house, alone. Jose was at work all day, and I was with Oliver and the other five children. This enforced seclusion was difficult for me, I had a restless, seeking spirit. Through Oliver, I was held still. I was forced to embrace a silence and a solitude where I could "prepare the way of the Lord." Sorrow opened my heart, and I "died." I underwent this death unaware that it was a trial by fire from which I would rise renewed more powerfully, more consciously alive. I looked into the

abyss of human sorrow and saw how dangerous and how easy it is to slide into self-pity, to weep over one's fate. I was given the grace to understand that one has to be on guard against such grieving, for it falsifies one's grasp on life and erodes one's inner strength... Looking at Oliver I saw the power of the powerless. His total helplessness speaks to our deepest hearts, calls us not merely to pious emotions but to service. Through this child I felt bound to Christ crucified, and also to all those who suffer in the world. While caring for Oliver, I also felt that I ministered, in some mysterious way, to all my unknown brothers and sisters who were, and are, grieving and in pain throughout the world. Through Oliver I learned the deepest meaning of compassion.

Catherine produced a sizeable body of poetry during those years. Most of her books of poetry were published by Alleluia Press (P.O. Box 103, Allendale, N.J. 07401). Nearly all of them have been reprinted. The Monks at Weston Priory use her work in their liturgies.

I know it gives Catherine great joy to present this selection of her favorite poems to you. She offers them with love.

Father John Catoir
Easter 1996

God of a Thousand Names

God of My Life

Sometimes, I hide your name
    like a piece of silver
      kept in a deep pocket of silence.
Sometimes, I wear it on my breast
    an abstract jewel, a disk
      engraved with letters I cannot read.
It glows on my flesh
    a red burning, a thumbprint of light.

Sometimes, your name flashes with star-fire
    through enormous distances.
I follow its trail
    even though, yes,
I am here, riveted to planet earth
    that small object of blue color
revolving through the galaxies
    spinning on and on
while I remain still
    at this desk, in this room;
while I speak it
    with living lips
      your name
        God.

Steady Light

*"God, how hard it is to grasp your thoughts; it is impossible to count them!
I could no more count them than I could the sand."* (Psalm 139:17-18)

*I*t falls away from me, that knowledge
　　　　even as it enters, passing
　　　　through the sluices of the mind
　　　　permeating my very substance.
So otherly other, it cannot be seen
　　　　yet it lies over me like a bridal veil
　　　　whiter than sister moon
　　　　lighter than sister snow.

I live inside that knowing
　　　　yet cannot trap it, cannot hold it
　　　　into a woven net of words
　　　　no matter how hard I try
　　　　to tighten the knots of metaphors.

How easy to define
　　　　the cascade of the wisteria
　　　　blue paradise for butterflies and wasps;
easy to learn the reality
　　　　of the maple leaves, each one
　　　　a map of small green rivers.

In the reliquary of memory
　　　　I keep bits of yellowed paper
　　　　printed with foreign phrases
　　　　stamped with images of people
　　　　of towns I hardly remember.

What enchants me today, life
　　　　worn like a golden tunic
　　　　will tomorrow hang in dusty rags
　　　　from my bony shoulders.

But neither present nor past
    can alter what forever endures:
    that steady light, beamed
    to the heart's core, yet impossible
    to confine within my narrow human reach.

What I know best, I know least.

The Fire Within
The Fire of All Things

I start here
　　　in the mud of the rainy season
　— the land's ragged fabric
　　　coarse under the probing hand:
brittle sedge, lifeless vine
　　　thorny twig of the vanished rose...
How far to the next road
　　　to the house of many lamps?
How far to the other side
　　　the place beyond history?

This is where it begins
　　　in this pattern, this path
　　　corrugated with deep ruts
where I wander in and out of step
　　　through the zig-zags of idle thoughts.
Here I advance, meeting the fox
　　　a quick flame flaring among the reeds.
I feel helpless
　　　dazed by such beauty.

Then I say to myself:
　　　If I can shiver with joy
when the wind rises
　　　puffed up, full voiced
to later fall back quietly
　　　folding itself pleat by soft pleat
　　　into a fluttering rag of air;
if I dance with happiness
　　　at the sight of the circling hawk

knowing for a moment what it is
    to float over the swamp
    in a robe of dark feathers;
and if I do hear the summons
    hidden within the miracle of stones:
then I can name the holy
    the Fire within the fire of all things.

Voice Rising
From the Dark

You are our dream, someone passing
    shadowless through our sleep
calling us with the voice
    of water and fire, of earth and air
naming us as the stars are named
    as the moon is set in motion
    to bloom in the spring night.

Inside the self lies a great knot
    a reptilian tangle: half-conscious
    half-formed riddles hidden from the light.
Like the wind, you sweep through our mind
    anesthetized by sleep
to reach that region deeper than the bone.

You are our dream
    moving through our fears
    pushing away their coiled hissing mass.
We hear it then, your voice
    rising from the dark,
    saying:
"Thou shalt not die."

Rock of Ages

"You are my rock, my fortress." (Psalm 7)

*F*oundation
    rock
        rock-bottom of our lives
    this is what you are:
a floor of hard granite over which
    we build our paper houses
    our castles in the air.
Building we do, walls and gates
    rooms to sleep and work and play.

Under our sorrow
    you are the buttress
    for centuries unmoved
while the torrents of history rush by
    with their cargo of blood.

In our speech of ever-shifting meaning
    you are changeless Verb,
    diamond Word
    writing itself on our tablets of clay.

When we scale the snowy mountain
    the heavy sack of our daily need
    slung over our shoulder
you are the foothold chiseled in the cliff.
At our right, at our left, the abyss yawns
    glacier of unfathomed depth
    calling us with its icy iridescent voice.

How we fear the timelong plunge
    the scream without echo
    the endless loss.

But our toes find the carved stair
    our fingers numb with cold
grasp the ledge, and we haul ourselves up
    step by step, moment by moment.

It is simple then to learn:
    your love is not soft and plump
    a cushion for our fall.
Underneath our trembling, our doubt
    it lies unchanging
    ancient as stone
    the ground of our strength.

Ancient Tower

"I am circling around God, around the ancient tower and I will be circling for a thousand years; and I still do not know if I am a falcon or a storm or a great song."
(R.M. Rilke, "The Book of Hours")

*T*he wings, two inverted commas
      printed on the vellum of the sky;
      the eyes golden, fixed in total attention.
I am a hunting falcon
      my feathered feet hide
      the horned curve of the claws.
Prince of the air, extravagant in power
      I circle the ancient tower.
The prey lies within
      — a kernel concealed in straw?

No, I am not a grain-eater
      I do not want that prize:
I want flesh and blood
      the heart of hearts of all things
      the pulsing sac, container of wisdom
      and of beauty and of ample truth.

I do not tire:
      following the rim of space
I soar above the land. I see
      at the mouth of the rivers
      clustered nests of people
      burrows of fishermen and traders.
I do not seek shelter:
      the rain presses its water-weight
      upon my back;
the snow falls around me
      in cascades of luminous blossoms.
I am a barbarian from the high sierras

wear a crested headdress
dance in the abyss
cry wildly, of desire and hunger
round and round the ancient tower.

The incantations I repeat
    the words I hurl about
    break on impact.
My tongue is an arrow
    behind the beak's armored plate
and if I have a mind
    it is a small room
crammed full of a single thought:
    God.

I do not tire:
    I am a plumed storm
    and yes, I am a great song.

The Word

*I*n the beginning
        a name was found for stone:
a sound — in what tongue —
        to keep it there, solid
in one place, a familiar sight
        a marker at the end of a field.

Names were found
        for what could be reached:
curve of apple, of cheek
        immediacy of bread
to say, "Yes, here it is
        under my hand, mind.
An anchor in this trembling map
        in this breaking web."

A name was found
        in the maze of connections
the child in us
        inventing it:
"God," we say, wrapping the word
        around our life
        a garment of mist
a cloudy fleece to ward off
the chills of perennial pain.

At last we dare to let go
        thoughts, images, loosened
shed like breast-feathers
        sloughed off like dead skin.
We enter the cave of silence:
        in darkness

with fingers of air, we touch the
    first-born of a language
    we cannot speak
and let our tears fall
    of diamonds and rosin
    before him in the straw.

"I AM!"

"Before Abraham came to be, I AM." (John 8:58)

So many years
      migrating through snow and wind
      leaving behind broken pots, torn rags
      the dead sewn in their cloaks.

So many years
      wandering in the tundra
      following injunctions, obscure urges
      feeling infinitely small, alone
      under the incomprehensible sky
      under clouds darkly packed
      built into a density of illegible signs.

So many years
      moving from one campsite to another
      carrying embers:
      the jewels of fire in iron boxes.

No one talks to us but the crows
      and they only in summer, after the hunt.
Further in the dream that is real
      the wolf speaks, and, in turn, the eagle;
down passages of time, closer, always closer
      to someone who is silent, yet ever sings;
      through the bodies of children
      through the bone configuration of women
      through the skin, the feet, the face
         of all that breathes
      someone sings:
         "I AM! I AM! I AM!"

Bread of Angels

"You gave them the food of angels from heaven, untiringly sending them bread already prepared, containing every delight, satisfying every taste." (Wisdom 16:20)

I hunger!
    Neither shamed nor cowed
my starved body craves for substance
    for answers in the shape of food.
I dream of enormous tables
    set with enormous dishes
and I, nothing but a ravenous mouth
    — one among many —
cracking marrow bones
    licking snowy alps of sugar
lapping ambrosia
    distilled from flowing sap.
I want my life cupped in bowls of grain
    condensed in the scent of herbs
their sweet names garlanded
    around the kitchen
rosemary and thyme
    parsley, marjoram, and chervil.

I hunger:
    my spirit blue with cold
dreams of a warm working-place:
    a great field, freshly plowed
    rows of seeds in damp earth.
How does one grow into the light
    open to the sun a greenhouse of leaves
become a poppy or a rose
    dressed in satin sheets?
My spirit hungers
    a thin ghost with slender fingers

needing to grasp some slivers of truth.
I do not wish to descend
     — by what dark ladder —
into the mossy well
     to reach many fathoms down
     some brackish muddy water.
I do not wish to enter the cave
     place of shadows, grey hollow
     for the final repose of mortal flesh.

At sunset
     the world rounds itself
     into a reed basket
holding five barley loaves
     two silvered fish pale as the moon:
not enough to feed the tribes
     reclining on the grassy slopes.
The Master of knowledge stands on the mound:
     at his feet
seas unfurl their ancient scrolls
     continents throb like murmuring hives.
I am, I am, I am crying out
     waiting before an empty plate.
Over the bread, over the fish
     he speaks the eternal blessing.
Now and forever, I, one among many
     take and eat, the basket never empty
       the gift never withdrawn.

Dancing Master

"Teach me how to dance." (Nikos Kazantzakis, Zorba the Greek)

A body mounted on pins
      hands and feet held still
      pulled open.

Under torture, you answer
      the voices that perpetually ask:
"Can you dance, can you move
      these arms, these limbs
not an inch or two
      away from the wood
but in a rising that lifts the world
      out of the jaws of death
brings song to dry throats
      skin to bleached bones?"

"Even the most distant planets
      the stars of gas and diamond
turn in my dancing,"
      says the Lord.

The Word Made Flesh

"And the Word was made flesh and dwelt among us." (John 1:14)

The stars speak
    in their Christmas tongues
hang their cold silver overhead.

How can this be taught:
    what the water says
    in its transparent running;
    what the earth hums
    in the labyrinth of its roots?

How can this be heard:
    these hosannahs
    sustained from age to age:
    voices of elephants and sparrows
    alleluias of luminous flowers
    white canticles of snowflakes and moonlight
    and the ever-rising chorus of leaves
    shaking green sounds into the air?

How can this be understood:
    she who has never known man
    — a singular woman, yet like any other
    rich in flesh and blood —
she breaks open: the child bursts forth
    wild and free, hearing within himself
    the chant of the seven seas
    the song of the whales
    the tumult of angels unrolling
    great banners of praise
and the immense concert of all the hosts
    heavenly and others, shepherds, wise men
    fools on every continent

singing day after day
as the blue planet turns
on the spindle of time:
    "Holy, Holy, Holy Lord
       God of Power
           God of Might!"

God of Our Hope

*"Awake, exult, all you who lie in the dust, for your dew is a radiant dew,
and the land of the ghosts will give birth." (Isaiah 26:19)*

*W*hat we leave behind:
    a land of small toys, of miniature trains
winding their way through open fields
    arriving at safe destinations
where people wait for us
    with ribboned gifts.

Here, on high ground, ice glazes the rocks
    a few twisted pines resist northern gales.
At night, instead of woolly sheep
    we count and name our losses;
gone the love-games, the playful hours
    gone the children picking flowers
floating over the garden
    like angels;
gone the daffodils
    shooting their green arrows
spring after spring
    in the same perennial spot.
Silence, in huge bell-spaces
    rings cool and ardent, of snow and sun.

Is there any time left?
    In the background
we hear the axer cutting fresh wounds
    in the flesh of the world's trees.
Shall the wolf survive, the wood violet
    the lotus and the tiger?
Shall there be a final meeting
    moments of perfect understanding
by the grave

out of which Lazarus slithers
changing skin, shaking the scales of death
from hands and feet?

We wait, hungering for further miracles.
Cities of hope lie in ruins;
rivers drag their long brown bodies
heavy with scum and sludge, to the sea.
We hunger for completion
the coming full-circle of our life:
birth-day touching death-day
clasping one another
closing the gap
as time collapses into a single compact:
one instant of many years
one moment into which we tremble
our pale moth-wings unfurling
opening slightly, slowly
readied for ascension and flight.

A Book of Uncommon Prayers

Cover Me With the Shawl of Prayer

"No, I shall not die; I shall live and declare the works of the Lord." (Psalm 118:17)

I speak to you:
  my mouth breathes
        the first letter of your ancient name
        forms the sound of forgotten words.
  I speak
        but less clearly than stones
        and with less excellence than rain.
  I am flesh of your flesh
        measured, poured out and recaptured
        in this cup of space
        this goblet of time.
  I share with others straw bed
        and hard pillow
        the casual babble of the world
        the multiple passages
        through which the mind
        — that poor dumb fish —
        swims in search of you.
  My body moves, not a blind shell, house
        of spirit lighter than my bones
        but a landscape of life:
        face, breast, knee pressed
        to the quivering ground
              I feel
        the dance of your footsteps
              shaking to life
        dead wood and frozen spring.

  Have mercy on me
        have mercy on these small gestures
        that give love, beg recognition.
              Cover me

with the shawl of prayer
and let my tears come to you
heavy and luminous as stars.
What is this web I meet
this net of mist
through which I see beyond sight?
Visible
among invisible threads
I struggle to force a way
of milk and light
to touch the source of you.

Break open, reach, lift.
My words are bells sewn
around ankles and wrists:
they ring, they call.
But only death has power, hook and crook
to haul me over the last wall:
one sweet leap, one final cry
and the voice drowns
the blood rests.

Teach Me How to Dance

"David and all the House of Israel danced before the Lord with all their might, singing to the accompaniment of lyres, harps, tambourines, castanets and cymbals." (2 Samuel 6:5)

*L*ife is a bed of roses
     a bowl of ripe cherries
         — Ha!
Long ago the flowers curled
to a papery death
blackbirds rifled the berry-tree
mindless of cat, bell and shouting child.

In the mirror of another time
     I look
showing myself uneasy
       coming
into history, ritual, rubble
asking, "Who am I?
        What images swim
        in these sealed depths?"
In the backroom of childhood
aproned mothers sit by the fire
their knees huge, their laps
throne or cradle. Further in time
earth-mothers squat on the cave's pitted rock
pounding grain, rolling clay in their palms
fashioning the future.

Here, among dishes and cups
     I sip the nectar of roses
     eat one sweet cherry
but
     life is a hard pallet in a cold night
sometimes
     at best

a place of white linen
a nest in which to dream the next question:
What to do? What to wear?
        Into what form to turn?
Mythologies, legends invent themselves
but I pound the words, crack their shells
cook their meat on the spit of my years.
Thus I survive
        by skill, by luck
        saved by art and grace
and I say
        God
        I delight in your work
        I have seen you in stick and stone
        my laughing God, Lord of the garden
        Father of power over seed and root.
From moment to moment
        invent my life
        Lord of movement and change
        invent me.
Gather the dusty sparrows of my days
hear them sing in your eternal branching.
        Pain, exile, hunger
        the bitter rains dripping through the walls
        the house stripped
        — I do not want a bed of roses.
Grass will grow
where beam upon beam, bone upon bone
        stand now in measured connection.
        — I do not want a bowl of cherries.
But, yes, invent my life, light
        a passionate fire
        a thing of blazing gold
and let me laugh in your joy
        my laughing God
and leap in your rising
        my Dancer!

I Hear a Manner of Answers

*"I tell you, therefore: everything you ask and pray for, believe that
you have it already, and it will be yours." (Mark 12:24)*

I ask
      and in my daily dust ask again:
Where is the way?
Does the knife know, the plow, the falling axe?
I dip the pen, begin to draw:
      beyond account, the line moves
      from a hilltop to a landscape
      of astonishing rocks.
Can I explain why the word stone
      drops on the page with a grey weight?
How the world's fragments speed
      dangerously about? Glass shards
      needles of perception break
      the skin, enter the brain.
Changes, miracles of invention
      build new shapes, new sounds:
      among the multitudes, the swarming choices
where is the guiding cord
      the single thought uncoiled
      from the tangled mess?

Intricate, voluminous
billowing around my ankles:
      a Japanese robe, a silken wrap
      such is my life; but who sees
      my iron shoes, the dark bruise on my flesh?
At the table of the world
I take and eat
      the sugar-cones of mountains
take and lift
      the steaming bowl of the sea.

But I still hunger, still fear:
    death is no sweet apple
    but a clustered thing hung
    at eye-level in the weighted tree.

God
    I ask again and again
    for I am this question
    screaming in your space:
    one among many, looking
    for the possible door, the answer
    carved into the ever-circling O
    of your peace.
Where are those who came before me:
    the people marching through sand-storms
    carrying the day's provisions
    a water-jar, a scroll
    a pot to cook the morning manna?

It so happens: today I am stranded
    among steel pipes and motor cars
    — but the crows in the oak tree
    are very old, and the wind
    from age to age drums
    the same message against the walls.
God
    the oracle speaks:
    your voice in pine and palm
    in fish-scale and bright coral;
    your prophecies
    in the veins of each leaf
    in bone and living face.
I hear it
    a manner of answer, a word
moving
    dark and quick
      behind the glass.

Death Has No Power

"The Lord says this: Come from the four winds, breath; breathe on these dead; let them live!" (Ezekiel 37:9)

*O*ut of its northern cave
    the wind blows, full-cheeked
        breathes ice on every earth-fold
           on every crease of stone.
  In our small web of flesh
     our bones tremble: we shake, draw back
     remember warmth of womb, shelters
     where constant fires keep watch.

Are we speaking? Words congeal in the air
     hang in white balloons of breath.
With our care and our seeking
     we wish to say: "All things are well;
     the day is a plaything, a rubber ball
        bounding on concrete, a reality
        of living equilibrium, repose and leap."
But we move with such speed, hurled
     forward from one winter to the next;
  our eyes like headlights probe the dark
     looking for clues. If greenness is to come
     we should hear the speech of roots
     the underground travail of springs
     the whispers of the dead.

What is it that we wish with such sighs
     such pain, such wildness of the mind?
Love, yes, love ascending
     through all the shapes of our dying
        — fearful thoughts nightly scuttle
     back and forth, tarnish the moon
     spoil the bread, sour the wine.

The northern wind seeps into cracks
    nails doors shut, blows lights out
    one by one. But we are here:
        we are now, our gloved fingers hold
        the hourglass through which time shifts
        and falls — and we laugh:

Father of rivers and frost
Father of birds, of children, of yes:
        we have heard the dust crying out
        and the sap of our life shouting
        louder and far beyond our death.

Have Mercy on Us

"Have mercy on me, O God, in your goodness, in your great tenderness, wipe away my faults; wash me clean of my guilt, purify me of my sin." (Psalm 50:1-2)

*I*n dark flashes, images fall
    melt in a rushing stream
    — fire or flood, we do not know.
Dressed in fallacies and frills
    we stand by the window, rubbing our eyes.
Colors drain from the morning sun;
the garden turns black that yesterday
    was painted with pink roses.

What is left? Amplified sounds
    scurrying rats in tapestries of garbage
    echoes of upturned pebbles.
In terror, the heart shrinks
    to a pulsing red dot.
Shall no crow with bread in beak appear
    no angel descend with pitcher and loaf?
— Habacuc of the stolen pot
    where are you with your soup?
We starve in the dark pit, weep
    find no companion but the rising wind.
There is nothing to say
    except yes, Lord, we are sinners
    and come to pray:
"Have mercy on us, O God
    in your goodness, in your great tenderness
wipe away our faults."

Ikon

The Mother of God

*L*ADY,
    silver mined in Israel,
daughter
    of the rich vein
      that courses through the land
daughter
    of the river
      that so briefly flowed in Eden;
        she surfaces now
her head clear,
    her limbs slowly disengaged
    from millennia of sleep.
She comes from the deep
    in a net of silver, held
    by silver ropes, hauled
    from the pit of history
    in one splendid blast of love.
She carries messages,
    scrolls unroll
      from her lips
and her language blazes in the shade of summer trees.
"The Lord possessed me
    in the beginning of his ways
before he made anything
    from the beginning."
She is with him
      when he stands on the shore
    of his own sea, letting the yeast of life
    rise through doors and windows of space
    forming a new body, a playhouse
    for the delight of his wisdom.

She is with him
        as he pulls the sun
        through the loops of her silver
lady of rings of beads of phosphorescent crowns.
     First woman
        silver-hammered in the beginning
        as the fire-tongue splits
        into many smaller flames
        into the rainbow variations of light.

Strapped to her deepest flesh:
        the child.
He moves from alpha to omega:
        a word that speaks, breathes
        seasons and tides
        rock leaf grass
     swooping bird leaping sea
       the pattern
       color
           throb of life.
She dances in the cave
dances on the silver floor of her mind,
her arms like wings,
her legs parted
as he comes from her
        burning: flame and light
        first cry of God
        and milk-drops falling
        through the sky
more radiant than stars.

It is cold in the barren hills:
       sand
       stones
       lizards
       scorpions
baked into a dry world

a small place lit
by dung fires.
What perfumes walled your sleep
Lady,
what silks trailed in the wind
to cover your head?
What do we bring to your feast
we of the faithless tribe, shepherds,
dubious kings, dwellers of nervous cities;
what herbs, what garlands,
what succulence for the sucking child,
what rainbow carpet
for the stairs of his wisdom?

GOLD   FRANKINCENSE   MYRRH

Here
at your feet
the ashes of Auschwitz
prayer shawls of old men, jewels
carved from the bones of Israel.
Here
your royal necklace, constellations
of David's children quivering
in the hiss of deep fires.
The seven-branched tree lifts
stems and flowers of smoke
drips with the wax of melted flesh.

"By the rivers of Babylon, we sat and wept."

Next year in Jerusalem, next year
by the wailing wall we shall meet
in a passion of tears.

Eyes of the dead
womanly thighs softer than bread, feet
following the beat of pastoral dances

expressive hands caught
in gestures of terror and grief:
          they rise
released like vapor out of the ruined wall;
          they speak
          they set their names
     in depths of time, recalled, recalling.

Next year in Jerusalem,
shall we know you then,
          Lady
as your lips touch the ancient signs
as we see your kiss take root and grow?

GOLD   FRANKINCENSE   MYRRH

The phantoms glide
butterfly-shadows across a paper door.
Hiroshima mon amour!
Small running figures suddenly break
into zones of absolute stillness;
they sail on the river of their blood
the coals of their eyes red-hot
the shape of their body melting
merging with air-currents, wind-curves.
Suspended in our blind skull,
bursting
     in our seeing dreams
the mushroom cloud proclaims
          the luck of the cockroach,
          the coming of the reign
               of deathless stones.

GOLD   FRANKINCENSE   MYRRH

The raped girl bleeds over Vietnam
the moon silver-slides over her wounds

high plateaus of cheeks
acres of breasts, hills and valleys
of oriental death.
Dashed to the ground
the ceremonial cup releases
sobs of children
wails of women
libations of rice-wine
poured on fresh graves.

Lady of Constellations

Lady of Constellations
remember our half-way house
the snake under the porch
the dragon in the orchard.
And how the heart explodes with wild desire
at the sight of the jeweled apple
— the seeds within are black
are tears.
The tree bristles
with lancet-leaves
flashes with diamonds and emeralds
while roots spring up, hook
our ankles, drag us miles underground
to a core and cave of death.
Further down
deeper
into the spiral of a time gone mad
the skull grins, the mummy adjusts its wrap
and in the empty cavern of the eye
a middle kingdom of dust
slowly
builds its temple.

Lady of the Cross
when the tongue fails
when words crack open
like frozen meatless fruits
when terror enters the brain
travels in the blood
screams and spills
through all the pores of the skin
come in haste
to the heaving hilly country of our need

come with hands cupped
to the shape of our pain
with feet like silver leaves
on the path of our weeping.
Come
with linen and oil
with the dazzle of all that is forged in fire
and burns toward morning.
Drive us out
of our midnight cell
where we fast
on tepid water
hard crust.
Drive us in the open
where the sun will sew our wounds
with golden threads.

COME
LEAD US HOME.

Poems of the Hidden Way

The Lord's Prayer

Our Father Who Art In Heaven...

*B*orn of sea-water, of blood
    we crawl on the beach
        wet, salted with early tears.
Above us, someone screams
        — the mouth of our first world closes.
Our back to the waves, we begin the journey:
        age after age, step after step
            we look for the ancestral home.
Is it here among the lilacs
        a garden where the heart-beat alone
            measures time?
No clock: only a pulse-count, a rhythm
        of moons and tides.
Or is it there, where we follow
        the logic of the hunt:
five hundred years through the continents
        hacking forests
        folding the jungle
            like a green ragged cloth
to come home to a room
        encumbered with machines
to come back
        to the same obsessive search?

Father
        we say Our Father
for we are many
        a tribe dispersed and assembled
           dressed in garments of earth
      shirted and shod in this web
        we call flesh. A sorry lot!

All night long we walked down the slopes
    through the junipers and the berry bushes
following one another in time
    son after father, daughter after mother
        carrying speech and skill.
But the past is a distant sound
    a muffled rattling in the ear.
What we said yesterday turns now
    into altered meaning.
We have lost the words
    flicked them off like gnats.
The tower we built, Babel-by-the-Sea
    — metal tongues ringing in a single shell —
        falls to a rusty heap.
From north to south
    the coastal towns are visited by plagues:
mushrooms in the rafters
sea-monsters in the wells
    the waters red and soured.

Father
    we have come this way and that
        buzzing with the rest of the swarm
        looking for what? We do not know.
Overhead, the sky curves like a roof:
    it is made of grey stone
        veined in gold and blue.

Father, we pray:
    a gift of sight enters the eye
    and we say: Yes!
in the time of trumpets and drums
    you are
        not the sum of all music
        but the one pure silence
        in which harmonies are heard.
In the time of darkness, of storm

you are
> not sun-king, lord of the rising day
> but that one pure source
>> from which light beyond light
>> eternally jets forth
>>> to burn into planets and stars.

Father
> we believe!

Hallowed Be Thy Name...

The temple stands four-square
> a place of candles and smoke.
We reach it after the trek
> through desert and grassy plains.
We bang on tambourines and drums
> pluck guitars, ring bells
>> — the clap, our will to praise
our metal voice striking
> the metal walls, crying:
>> "The temple of God
>>> the temple of God
>>>> the temple of God!"

It is not enough.

There are powers hidden
> in the sap of plants
> in the veins of stones.
There are secrets written
> within the hands
>> in these lines long and short
>>> criss-crossing the palms:
>> a geography of roads
>> a map constellated with blood.

49

We come to the temple dressed and feathered
covered to the eyes
          with all we are not.
We fear to say:
          I am man, I am woman
naked, mortal, dying
          with the long death that begins
                    at birth.
What we call life
          is a bluish flame
          sputtering in the dark.
The wick of our days blackens
          the wax melts and drips.

We cannot turn
          cannot forget we are in the flesh
                    scarred and suffering;
          cannot reject what is stamped on the mind:
                    the dreams of the race
          the eternal delight
                    of that rounded body we call earth
                    of that glittering star we call sun.

We are children
          of what we see and touch and drink:
we are earthlings
          brother to the fire
          sister to the water
          kin to the lion and the shark.

Father
          to hallow your name
we have words marking time
          rising from the ground of our lives
words for peach-blossom, eyelash, cloud
          for the joining and the parting
          for the coming-as-you-are

into this place, this temple of everywhere
open to the four winds
where we can say in fleshed spirit
in spiritual flesh:
"HOLY HOLY HOLY
is your name:
FATHER!"

Thy Kingdom Come...

All things move forward, then withdraw:
the hand, the eyes open and close;
the word pulled by its own weight
falls back, returns to silence.

And where are we going?
The wood-demons crack branches
split logs
walk heavily on the ground.
They will come, the foresters
bearing their load
ready with flint and steel.
And shall it all go up in smoke
the solid house
the well-rooted life
the bright flesh?

We move into the stone of the years
we chisel, we crack the rock.
In the half-dark of the cave
voices speak of love, ask questions
say, "How do you do" to strangers
who answer, "Fine, fine!"
while death coils itself
around their throats.

Where are the kings and queens
        the heirs to the Kingdom?
Children go forth from us
        claiming the moon:
they fill their pockets with moon-chips;
        weightless, suspended among the stars
they dance, they sing in the great void,
        but not for long:
the years stand at their back
        by the thousand
        spelling history and death.
They must return to the room
        where objects are still
        where small lamps give off
            small auras of light.

The Kingdom is within:
        this is the news we learn
            on the stretch of road
                we travel alone at the latest hour.
Could this be, we wonder
        all there is to find, to cherish, to know?
A dark homeland, a fixed landscape
        the night crunching underfoot like glass?
The Kingdom is within
        deeper than knowledge
            a place beyond all heights and depths.

We come to it, are led to see:
        we own ourselves, we are real;
        we need not fear the wood-demons
            polishing their axes.

"Lord, thy Kingdom is here:
        let us come into its peace!"

Thy Will Be Done On Earth As It Is In Heaven

Lord, you wrote it
    on the rock and on the tree
    in the lettering of a billion stars
    in the fold of a billion years:
time set upon time, age over age
    the days like pages opened
        to ancient baffling script.
We cannot read it; our eyes are hooded
    with membranes of sleep.
Dreaming, we move into the world
    feeling our way
        through what seems cold and hot
            dry and wet, sweet and sour.
We sow and reap, our minds scuttle
    through the fields like mechanical reapers
        cutting this and that
            the cockle and the wheat.
We pack and store:
    winter is always at the door
        a cold beggar, blue-fingered and hungry.
Our cupboards bulge
    our closets are full of facts and fancy.
Yet, when the table is set
    we find only bitter herbs in the dish
        ashes on the water
        dark flakes floating in the cup.

Lord, our flesh dreams softness
    dreams silk
    wishes your will easy
to go on the road, traveling easy
    on padded shoes.
Why are the streets iced over?
    Why do we fall in the white morning
        fall awake, roll out of bed

into a hard world slicked over
with pain?

We look all the way back to the beginning:
the cave as nursery
the fire as first guardian
spirit of the place.
We are sucklings at the breast:
the earth-mother teaches
the way of the buffalo
the manner of the corn.
We are slow movers: we lack skill;
we live distracted, too pressed
to feel life living in us
— a power of lilac and sun.

Father, let us see
the full text of your will
as it is here, now
drawn clear to the inner eye
a thing of beauty
a power calling us
to joy.

Give Us This Day Our Daily Bread...

Clear a field in the mind
plow deep
make pockets in the ground
to fill with the seeds of compassion.
Our lives lead nowhere unless they connect
one to one, one to many;
unless we say: "Take and eat
this is my own substance.
Drink, this is the spring

born of caring, the silver strands
passing through the fingers
flowing, always on-flowing."

Out of fear, we store, we safe-keep
while elsewhere actual people die
propped against thorn-trees
near the carcasses of their cows.
Ivory, the bones
delicately curved
ideally empty!
The wind blows
through the eye-sockets
the sand fills the corridors of the skull.

We come awake to the smell of coffee.
The queendom of the kitchen swells
with colors and scents.
We reach for warm, motherly food
soft to our soft gums.
The kettle whistles, milk is poured
the sugar travels through the blood.
Underground, pots and pans
still black with clinging soot
lie with ancient dead.

Will today's full cup
be found in a thousand years, broken
on the site of a ruined town?
We drip with juices, papaya's, pear's
the yellow of lemons, the red of berries
picked at an early hour
at the edge of the woods.
But something eludes us, we know not what
an essential grain, a single kernel.

Give Us This Day Our Daily Bread

the fat of the land, the corn
pounded on the stone
the mint, the anise, the fennel and the rue.
Yes, over the flames, the soup pot
the roasting meat.
Yes, in the hands of children
the sugar-stick, the buttered bread
yes!

But more:
the work has not ended:
we are not so confused as to say
"Enough, it is enough
when the dish is full."
There is an ultimate response
a word we need, a truth
to feed earth-sucking lips
to fill our own living hunger
that cries and begs:
"Give us today the answer to all seeking":
here and now
let us sit at the table of the world
the board rugged
scratching the resting arms
but the wine-jars ever filled
the loaves ever-multiplied
and our own selves, a space contained
in space without end.
How real is this? the heart knows
the pulsing blood speaks.

Forgive Us Our Trespasses…

Look at us, soft-gathered
    around a trembling center:
can we be anything but wanderers
    changelings pressed
        by time-changes, body-changes
            through places of drift and flux?
So, over and again
    "Farewell, sweet prince!"
We fold our tent, move on
    through the rise and fall
        the dust of hazy hills.

Look at us: we hang in orbit
    weightless.
We have made it
    the impossible journey
    the visit to the Sea of Tranquility
        to the waterless bed.
Ah, for what? In her lighted temple
    the moon calls for rituals
        pulls our tides
            with implacable hands.

Ah, for what?
We do not even know
    the stranger dwelling in our clothes
        living our life, dying our death.
We are shadows of shadows
    children of the dark side of the street.
Our own secrets are hidden:
    we see only by earth-light
    we struggle to keep ourselves awake
        attuned to gravity
            in power.

Have pity on us who are pitiful!
Yes, we bottle our tears,
Yes, we flaunt our wounds.
We are babes in a deep wood
wailing for Mama
big, beautiful Mama
with sugar-breasts
and arms like warm pillows!

Have mercy on us who are sinners!
In us, through vast dream-plains
powerful animals are hunting.
Wild beyond caution, they run
fitting our bodies to their wishing.
Hands unshape themselves
slip into fur and claw;
jaws grow huge: caverns of appetite
hungering for meat.

Instructed by dark beasts, we hunt
sweeping across the earth
leveling cities
pouring salt on good fields
ripping the forests open.
The beasts stir in us;
they wear our faces like masks.

Lord, have mercy on us now
and at the hour of our death!

As We Forgive Those Who Trespass Against Us...

Our eyes burn
so intensely they see
that one Man:

He lies stretched over the continents
    scarlet threads are pulled
        through his hands and feet;
his limbs drip blood over Asia
his open wrists pour over South America
    the wounds in his back ooze
        over the night-lands where we struggle.

We touch cold iron in the dark:
    stove without fire, pot without meat
    water-pipes dry and rusty.
Who has done this to us
    taken away the sweet rain
    the bounding deer
    the oil and the coal?
Why do we starve?
Why, why, why do we thirst?

"Forgive," he says
    "learn the difficult skill!"
Can we shake the bees of anger
    stinging the memory
    pumping venom in the mind?
Can we forget the hooks, the ropes
    the dangling lures — little mirrors
        in which we lost our way?
He bleeds over cities and fields:
    large drops fall, pool in the cracks.
"Drink that wine," he says
    "drink the power of mercy!"
We let it flow within.

Heavy, they are stone-heavy
    those we carry.
The very smell of their clothes
    their very touch

fill us with revulsion.
They have driven us in chains
across water-miles;
they have herded us like cattle
they have kicked us
broken our teeth
— we speak through wired jaws
see through gauzy patches;
we walk on crutches
but we carry them
our brothers, our sisters;
we hold them who need to be held
in pardon and mercy.

For millions of years
cycle after cycle
the sun has risen full;
for millions of years
life on this planet pulses
waxes and wanes like the moon.
All things fall to fatten the soil
but that one presence remains:
that one risen Man saying, "Peace
love your enemy
do good to those who hate you
forgive
and you shall be forgiven."

Let Us Not Fall Into Temptation...

They are so many:
creatures of the deep
rising sweet-voiced
lifting themselves

out of the waves
illusions caught in scales and fins.

We have come to the sea-mouth:
the air stinks of fish.
On the beach,
the jelly of the dying medusa
shivers blue and green.
At our back, the land grows ripe
the fruit hang in the trees:
plum, apple, the succulence of flesh
belonging to others: we cannot touch!
Before us, the liquid mother
filled with froth, full of food
glutted.

We sit on the sand
hear beyond the laughing gulls
the sound of plucked strings: lute?
Ancient music drifts in the wind
floods us with longing;
thousands of hands finger our clothes
tug at the hem of our coat;
nails lightly scratch our naked throat;
we are hot;
we fear what lives in the mind
that trapped power within the skull
that monster ready to tear
to thieve, to kill.
We, it is we whose faces appear
in the comic books:
dwarfs and giants
mermaids and mermen
lifting themselves — raw, untender —
from the pages
chanting their sad song.

If that pain were to last
        and anger not lie down
            like a dog exhausted
                from too much barking
and if lust were not to break itself
        — an earthen cup
            flung against eternal rocks —
        then what?
The old stories are about death:
        they repeat themselves.
Year after year
        they bring images of boats
            sailing dark on darkening waters
            sailing down around the capes
                where perpetual winds blow
                full-cheeked
                    spinning the hulls mad.

Father, lead us away from the bitter waters
        from the home of turbulent spirits
into a garden, a place of hushed voices
        where tamed beasts lie on flagstones
            their golden eyes, half closed
                in deep rest!
Father, no more raging
        no more bonfires over which to leap
        no more rocking by the sea-mother
— she wept in our tears
        called in the very salt in our blood.
No more!
        Receive us in your peace!

But Deliver Us From Evil...

Deliver us from the evil
　　that grins through the teeth
　　　　glows through the slit of the eye.
Yes, we shall spit it out
　　we shall weep ardent tears
　　　　say we regret — but again and again
we find ourselves surprised:
　　in the dark of the mind
　　in the cave
murderous words crouch and wait.

We make, we destroy;
　　weapons are stockpiled
　　bombs hang like eggs
　　　　in the claws of the soaring eagle.
We give birth, sing lullabies:
　　elsewhere, we kill the child
crossing the footbridge
　　in the wrong time in a year of war.

Deliver us from evil!

Legions, they are legions:
　　like horsemen, they ride in the wind
　　　　dressed in steel shells
　　　　　　clanging with spurs and swords.
They rip through the pages of history
　　stuff the word "death" into time's cracks
　　spreading foul scents over the land.
There are radiant faces lightly borne
　　on long-stemmed bodies:
flowering girls
　　shining young men.
But the monstrous army comes in
　　bitter-strong, whipping the lights out.

Voices in the city
a running of voices
a bleeding of sounds!
Why are mothers with leaking breasts
weeping?
Why are babies still?

Deliver us:
it is late in the day
near evening maybe on the cosmic clock
— centuries are minutes
raining into space.
What have we done all time long?
Sold what belonged to others?
Chosen cowardly silence?
Forsaken the poor?

Deliver us from evil:
from the glut and the smell
of bulging cupboards
of closets where we store
more than we need.
Turn the mind, that strange stone
to the fire-light of your truth.
Let us invent something new
a new way of seeing, of knowing, of being.
Let us begin to be human!

For Thine Is The Kingdom And The Power And The Glory

We move by sight, by touch
in enormous rooms
Rivers and seas lap at the threshold:
what do we know?
Six hundred generations

since the Egyptians:
how many since the raw beginning
since the yolk of life oozed
into the blank void?

The time-clock ticks on
recording wars, death-marches
plagues and famines.
Onward we go, moving by touch
by sight
bumping into the furniture:
the towers we built
the temples on the hills
the columns, altars and thrones.
We are many, we are alone
we walk deeper into the cold
— it is winter on the plains:
a new ice-age stills the waters
freezes the flames.
We shiver, isolated machines
engines pumping heat
to the surface of the skin.
Father, we need you
we call from the distance where we crouch:
small men and women lost
in great cavernous depths.
Our words echo ancient runes
retell ancestral lore.
Figures on the wall leap
as in a dance
run with antlered beasts.
We are the same people
image-makers
hunters
inventors of the fire;
we call you with one voice

from these enormous rooms
   where the sound rubberballs
     from moment to moment
     from century to century
      repeating:
         THINE IS THE KINGDOM
         AND THE POWER
         AND THE GLORY!

Peace Cantata

Commissioned in 1984 by Regis College (Weston, MA) with the assistance of a New Works Grant from the Massachusetts Council on the Arts and Humanities. Music for organ, brass, tympani, narrators and chorus composed by Emma Lou Diemer. Premiered at Regis College, April 18, 1986 under the direction of Sheila Pritchard Vogt.

*I*n the beginning was the Word
      Word of peace
      spelled in syllables
      of water and earth
      fire and air
      rising like music
through the roots of all things
      composing this planet
      into a place of history
      house of open doors
      space fit for living.

In the beginning
      in time's first turn and shift
man, woman, apart and together
      found intonation, voice
      to name the wonder
      of stone and light and wind.

Later
there was a village, a neighborhood
      people clustered in small rooms
      sharing food, holding in common
      language and lore
      following the roll and pitch
      of sea and moon.

Not all at once, but slowly

pulling threads of coarse fiber
"we can wait a little longer
we can linger and pretend
life is but a silver stream
on which to row our boat
our precious private ark
        gently, safely
out of sight, out of reach."

❊   ❊   ❊

Now, the drumbeat of language
counts profits, programs facts:
        mega-dollars
        mega-bombs
        mega-deaths.
Isn't everybody doing it?
        Selling by the pound, by the hour
        by the time we reach the docks
        where tall ships are bringing in
            coffee and slaves?
Isn't everybody doing it?
        Marketing, buying
        the lives of those who labor
        in cane fields, in tea plantations
        those who weave basket and cloth
        those who scrape the desert floor
        for crumbs fallen from our table?
            "PEACE, PEACE, PEACE"
        we chant in the early dawn.
The words fall like snow
        settle in public places
        but they freeze on the ground
as the clanging of cymbals increases
        announcing death-without-end.

Oh, say, can you see
>the plague in the well
>the rot in the landfill
>the chained barrels in the sea?

Oh, say, can you see
>Guernica, Auschwitz, Babi-Yar
>Rome burning, Jerusalem sacked
>Troy the fallen
>lying broken under the sand?

And, before that
>the striking fist
>the hurled rock
>Abel bleeding in the field?

Oh, say, can you see
>all the nameless places
>nameless people
>ground like stone
>returned to gravel piles
>>to lime pits?

Who shall tell us
>the shape of time to come
>if our days are no more
>than a fluttering of wing
>a brief pulsing in the air?
Who shall bring us
>beyond the darkening zone
>of no corn, no apple
>no man's, no woman's land?

What will happen
>if the text of our story blurs
>on the page of creation
>leaving no trace in the radioactive ash?

At every juncture of history
      armies are on the march.
Can we be heard above the din
      above the roar of time spiraling
      down the ages
      turning from dust to dust?

It is late:
      four minutes to midnight
      if we dare to look at the clock.
The weight of darkness bends us
      to the ground of our weeping.
We kneel
      at the gates of deserted houses
      at the border of no-trespassing;
we kneel
      before our brothers and sisters.
Touching the hem of their garments
      we ask forgiveness
      Nagasaki, Hiroshima:
a hundred thousand killed
      by a single bomb
a hundred thousand
      injured or missing!
We ask forgiveness
      we kneel in the cinders
      we beg for mercy.

                        ❈   ❈   ❈

Again and again, we wonder:
      what more can we do?
The echo of the question returns to us
      thinned to a needle of sound
and we are pricked, we are stained
      with the blood of our anguish
      of our doubt.

We may have another year
        we may have a minute or two:
who knows when the calendar will melt
        into a blank space
        a place of no witness
        no mother or father
        no lover or friend
no tree shining with a green light
        no stone left unturned
        no fragment of a word
        left to say, "Love!"
        to name innocence and mercy.

※   ※   ※

In deep silos of fear
        the bombs rest, shining eggs
        laid in the underground
        ready to hatch
        to release their plagues.

It is time to rise
        to free the long scream
        trapped for decades in our throats.
It is time to shout:
        "STOP!"
        Stop the obscene breeding
        the maggots implanted in our soil!
Stop the magicians, the yea-sayers
        stop the lullabies they hum
        to put our vigilance at rest.
What is left to us?
To invent a new story
        a new way
        of being on this earth,
        of being together

71

forming one luminous body
    one sacred flesh
    smooth, healthy
without remembrance of scars.

❊   ❊   ❊

Pilgrims of space
    we walk on the moon
    wander among numberless mysteries.
Yet our home is here, is now
    in the lands outspread around us
    in widening arcs of color:

AMERICA, AFRICA, ASIA
EUROPE, OCEANIA, ANTARCTICA
    ALL
    linked like syllables of one text
    like voices responding each to each
    distinct, yet equally sustained
        in the one same song.

It is time
    to honor our common work
    to choose light over darkness
        love over hate
        peace over war.
It is time to honor our bodies
to set warm flesh against the destroyers
    to say, "NO! You shall not pass!"
    You shall not trespass
    on the holy ground of our living.
You shall not tear the seamless robe
    you shall not kill the child
    neither in the womb
    nor on some foreign street.

It is time to ring the bells
        to announce a seventh day of rest
        a Sun-Day of celebration.

                    ❊   ❊   ❊

We can still make it
        gather the threads, the pieces
        each of different size and shade
        to match and sew into a pattern:
                Rose of Sharon
                Wedding Ring
                Circles and Crowns.

We can still listen
        to children at play
        their voices mingling
        in the present tense
        of a time that can be extended.

"Peace," we say
        looking through our pockets
        to find the golden word
        the coin to buy that ease
        that place sheltered
        from bullets and bombs.

But what we seek lies elsewhere
        beyond the course of lethargic blood
        beyond the narrow dream
        of resting safe and warm.

If we adjust our lenses
        we see far in the distance
        figures of marching people
        homeless, hungry, going nowhere.
Why not call them
        to our morning of milk and bread?

The coming night will be darker
    than the heart of stone
    unless we strike the match
    light the guiding candle
    say, "Yes, there is room after all
      at the inn."

           ❊   ❊   ❊

Listen!
    Even in the dark
    the leaves make a green sound:
    even in silence
    the stones speak a holy name
    and year after year
    the earth proclaims glory and peace
      if only we are of good will.

Listen!
    Something strains to be born
    to shake itself free:
    something brand new trembles
    at the far edge of our minds:
    the shape of a world to come
    conceived in our present labor and pain.
In the distance ahead of us
      people
    of different voice and tone and rhythm
    are gathered in the one great sound
    the life-sound of the future.

Already now
    in our flesh and bone
    we carry blueprints, charts.
The lines each in its proper place
    intersect to form diamonds and prisms
    new patterns of harmony.

Already now
　　　lifted by the strength of our hope
　　　we dance
　　　centered in the music
　　　　　in the light
　　　seeing with new eyes
　　　singing with new lips:
　　　PEACE, PEACE, PEACE
the luminous word that was
　　　in the beginning
　　　　　is now
　　　and ever shall be
in the freedom of our hearts
　　　word without end:
PEACE, PAIX, PAZ, PAX, SALAAM, SHALOM!

For My Son Oliver

(April 20, 1947 - March 12, 1980)

I keep still:
>   The word "death" forms itself
>   — a bubble in your mouth —
>   pushes itself clear
>   through your lips
>   screams red into the room.

It is noon: time is a hurled stone
>   a meteor of unknown substance
falling fast, shattering
>   the glass shell of the mind.
A splinter of hard brilliance
>   finds, under the breastbone
>   the trembling place: my heart.

Once more, I lean over
>   kiss your face.
Your body now a glacial ridge
>   a mystery
removes itself at increased speed
>   further and further away from me.

Perspectives shift
>   alter the March light
as it pours, milky white
>   through the window.
The trees, polished by the sun
>   shine like tin
the same trees
>   seen yesterday less sharply.

From the fixed ground of your dying
>   I hear the sound of working roots

of seeds breaking open to release
     stems of greening life.
Now your limbs slip out
     of icy winter wraps;
now the scaly buds of your eyes
     open into iris-blue flowers
and you wake to sight never seen
     as I return to strict necessity
to a world of doors and clocks
     of banked fires sending out
     feeble messages, sparks and smoke.

The Burial

(May 17, 1980, at the Priory in Weston, Vermont.)

*T*hey are burying
>   the small treasure of his hands
>   the bread of his flesh
>   now hard and stale.

The earth is open:
>   a gash, bleeding stones and sand.

I am
>   alive by the grave
feel my mouth warm and moist
>   — the tongue moving in its cave
>   forming words, taming
>   what wildly circulates in the blood
>   the scream of all that dies in pain.

>   They are letting him down.

How easily the cargo of his years
>   slips into the underground.
On the river of the dead
>   the oarsman is masked;
his dog barks silently
>   in the shadows.

I am aware of the body:
>   beneath my dress
my limbs, my breasts
>   the central place of the womb.
I imagine the darkness within
>   the soft pillowed place
where yesterday the child hung
>   ripe, heavy as a pod.

Between time and time
    life is ground fine
    a powder of ashes and roses.

I do not weep:
    this hole is empty
    but for tree-roots and bones.

Lord of the Living
    receive my son!

Litany of the Name of God

What is God like?" asks a child
    a question that must wander forever
    homeless in a landscape of silence.

    BUT
THE NAME OF GOD is sewn in my pocket
    a gold coin saved in a time of war.

THE NAME OF GOD is carved on my chest
    a seal on my heart, red hot, burning.

THE NAME OF GOD is a piece of paper
    stained with tears, scribbled
    with words of an unknown tongue.

THE NAME OF GOD dances on the ground
    in a thousand feet of joy.

THE NAME OF GOD is a waterfall
    crashing down from infinite heights
    bursting forth in angel-wings of foam
    then pooling gently in the hollows
    where women, mothers of the corn
    mothers of the barley and wheat
    wait with empty jars.

THE NAME OF GOD is a round chamber
    a womb where the world is born
    steaming, luminous, a body
    turning in measures of time.

THE NAME OF GOD is tattooed
    on the skin of the lion

on the membrane of the bat.
It is threaded through the clouds
with every ray of light.
It is the throbbing center
of all that travels the sky
day and night in constant spiraling:
planets, constellations, moons
and the widespread glittering zodiac
configurations beyond numbers.

THE NAME OF GOD is the hub
of time's wheeling sequences
age upon age of ice, iron and silver
incised in stone and star.

THE NAME OF GOD flows, energy of the sap
from root to flower, shaping
the wild rose full of ecstatic bees.

THE NAME OF GOD is a seed
buried in depth of plant life
in mysteries of trees, in the pulse
of lovers wedded in the hallel of their joy.
It grows, inviting birth, inventing
new patterns, new ways to attain
the moment of ripeness, the fruit.

THE NAME OF GOD bleeds
in newspapers and magazines:
Here, in close-up, a dead soldier
his eyes enormously open; there
a little girl shot in her crib
and further south in the sierras
Indians hung on butcher hooks
tormented for justice' sake.
The face of Christ looks on
through spittle and blood

at the incandescent bloom exploding
over Hiroshima, at the flesh
swollen with plagues, at the minds
invaded by parasites of fear.

What color THE NAME OF GOD
in Auschwitz, El Salvador, Guatemala
in Soweto, Tel Aviv and Baghdad?
Bright red, screaming red
pouring from the lips of the dying.

In the theater of the absurd
THE NAME is seldom spoken:
the actors eat, walk, sleep
respond to touch and kiss
follow signals of simple feelings.
Sometimes they remember a line
a lost word of significance
and THE NAME rises in their throat
as they plead in urgency, in hunger.

THE NAME OF GOD is a music room
a cave of resonance filled
with whistles, whispers, songs
with choirs of morning birds
rising crested and feathered
from the one great egg of creation.
Voices chant to the eternal reaches
seldom in harmony, but connected
word by word of every tongue
speaking the same beloved nouns:
mother   father   daughter   son
sister   brother. The sounds
lifted from the four corners
in rhythms, syncopations, drumbeats
mingle high and low, praising.

THE NAME OF GOD is a flying shuttle
        weaving, weaving without pause
        the broken threads, the pitiful fragments
        all the loose, the lost ends, lives
        thrown away on the scrap-heap
        but retrieved, redeemed, restored
        to the loom where the final tapestry
        unrolls its luminous sequence.

THE NAME OF GOD is the bronze door
        of God's household. On the panels
        figures of guardians, prophets and saints
        with living faces, living hands
        beating hearts. Around the lintel
        a vine grows in convoluted branching:
        image of life in its timeless leaf and bloom.
        From the underworld, grimacing spirits
        bring tools forged in darkness.
        Their armies obscure the sun
        poison the air, ravage the land.
        They fail to break the holy door
        they retreat, ghosted in their vanishing.

THE NAME OF GOD is a city on fire
        and I, within, choke and weep
        until I understand: I am called
        to be robed and shod in flames
        to let my tongue speak hotly
        to rejoice in an ardor without end.

THE NAME OF GOD rings
        in all the towers of the world
        a bell to wake the sleepers
        its sound, without angles
        smooth and round in its rolling.
        It enters all dwellings, hovers

under the eaves. It forms itself
into familiar tones and colors:
white notes of snow, green of rain
pastel tinkle of flowers
golden cracking of thunder.
Deep in the heart of themselves
the dreamers hear at the edge of sleep
the bell's dominant voice
calling them to the universal feast:
on the table of the world
loaves of bread, multiplied and warm.
It is Easter morning —
    and the bell rings.

Hope

Now that life itself is flattened
      pierced by nails, wreathed in thorns
  now that your own body falls
     soft and limp into empty space
       — nothing to catch, no foothold
        no ledge
only white emptiness
    through which you descend:
the ground comes closer
    the hard stony earth looms larger.
Already you imagine your bones broken
    your hands useless, your life crushed.
Just before you are to hit rock-bottom
    a small parachute of hope opens
    a corolla with filaments of light
and you are held, you swing free
    from deadly gravity:
you float in azure currents
    through lanes of air
through wide avenues of pure ozone
    and go on living another day.

A Liturgy

In the name of the Father
and of the Son
and of the Holy Spirit

Father
    we confess:
          in our gloved hands, claws;
          under our eyelids, raging seas
            shipwrecks, depths
      of dark and whirling thoughts.

In our breath, words break
            into glass shards
and our skull houses kingdoms of dust
        hollow chambers where the viper

nests
         where its young suck strange milk.
Lord have mercy!
      We are thieves in the night
      plunderers of the orchards:
      the world bears the mark of our teeth
      the shadow of our steps.
We steal
    what could be born to us:
the fire of gods, the torch that now clings
         to our flesh, a garment of flame we
cannot shed
       a burning fleece we cannot shake.

Christ have mercy!
Remember the dark of the earth
        which we call night, that time of the moon
        when we float with all dormant things
        on blind rivers of sleep.

Remember the orb of silence around us:
yes, they enter our lives
                    the sounds of turning wave
                        pressing wind,
but our true words bounce back
return to us without answers.

> *Lord have mercy on us*
> *forgive us our sins*
> *and bring us to everlasting life.*

We tell time, wear it
                    strapped to our wrist, hear
                        the minutes tap against our bones;
but what we count in months
                    in years
escapes our grasp, flows coil upon coil
into the grass, a serpent of slithering days.
                    Where
                        do we begin
and to what end do we so quickly move
to tell what tale, to leave what script
what small diffused light?

                    ❊   ❊   ❊

Lord of Glory
> *we worship you*
> *we praise you*
> *we give you thanks.*

Through a chink
                    of suddenly bright glass
through a crack in the last wall
                    at the back of our mind
we now dazedly see:
                        the one leaf grows into a forest

flames leap
from a single prong of fire
the only visible face
widens
into an immense crowd: men, women walk the earth
each one amazing
each one for a moment caught
in slow motion
on a screen of cosmic size and grandeur.
Slowly above the horizon line
they rise
stems and corollas of life
washed by the lapping tides of the ages.

The seamless curve they trace
begins in a distant dawn:
a thousand years is like a day
and a day like a thousand years;
the moment breaks to re-form itself
to extend the luminous sequence;
golden seeds fall into golden furrows
the rusted arrow flies into the future
flakes of rain wake the desert
reach our thirsty roots;
what fades reappears
what dies is born anew.
Lord,
on the ground
where your rain sings with crystal voices
we kneel to praise you
to give you thanks
for your great glory.

❋   ❋   ❋

Credo

I believe in my own existence:
my body breaks through the air
takes space, sets shadow and print
on earth   water   sky.
In the house of mirrors
at the fair
       I saw my image
trapped in crystal
          gliding on silvered walls
multiplied   divided   folded over and again
upon its own sum,
      as the fanned mirror narrowed
      and clicked shut.
I believe
    in my own reality
    — who is she, who, rising
    from glacial depths of glass
    has power of presence, of change, of speech —
Images of silver   paper   brass
    lie:
but I see   I am seen
I touch   I am touched
      by arms   mouth   hair
      by leaf feather fur;
I hear the caroling bird
    clear like a bell;
out of the narrowing circle
      let me spread my life
like a shimmering cloth
a satin that catches light at every move.
    Turn
    the lock of my eyes
    the key of my mind;
open the last invisible exit

at the back of my life, that I may see
that I may enter paradise
where all voices mingle as one:
rain-voice   milk-voice   whispering voice of light.
Open to me
        drive forth my true image
press me into my true shape
at last   at last   after so many breaking changes
        so many agonies of profuse choices
        so many voyages.
I believe in the hard mystery of a Church
half-wrecked with age
yet rising
        stone upon brilliant stone
                opal   diamond   ruby   emerald
        a tower of gems   a jeweled house
        spire higher than knowledge
        body filled with exuberant life
        emblazoned with stars that continually grow
        in size and splendor....
I believe in the resurrection of the flesh.
        Death
        shakes an iron rattle to my ear
        plays a flute of bones
        in the room where I am writing.
But I catch another tune
        a music to which I rise to dance:
Christ the Dancer takes my hand
leads me in the cadence and pattern
of a new language I learn as I go.
I pass from one rhythm to another
released from what restrains and cripples
to the ease of a space that unrolls
farther than my strongest thought.

I believe in oneness
        in the final wedding of all that is:

here   there   in surprised moments
taste and bliss are pressed
upon my blind and walled form
and I feel the thread of life pulled
through the fabric of the world
gathering all things
all ages of man   moon   earth
all students   servants   lovers of the truth
into a single shimmering cloth.

I live
live on
live forever
with this particular face
this body   shape   speech
merging with the Dancer
raised into the dance that he is
entering the wave of a music
that continually breaks
endlessly expands
into crescendos of light.
I Believe!

❈   ❈   ❈

Offertory

*"Blessed are you Lord of all creation:
through your goodness we have this gift to offer."*

A meteor
hurled in the night
from age to age
a planet balled in blue light
spinning in the swarming hive of space.
We creep over the surface

91

holding on to what we know:
>the egg that fits the hand
>the ripe flesh of the peach
>the moment at sunset

when the wild geese lift their voices
above the water
when the reeds softly speak to the wind.
Our minds cannot contain the final sky
>the absolute chasm above our head.

Our sight enters the emerald glow
>of hemlock and pine
>but cannot follow the sunray
>to the white medusa of heat
>pulsing on a fiery beach
>thousands of years away.

Lord
>we are thankful
>>for the scale of what we touch:
>>snowflakes float
>>small, harmless, to our hand.

Yet as they reach our deepest gaze
>they loom wide, build crystal caves
>in which our thoughts begin to freeze.

Lord,
>we bring you what we are:
>>creatures of transit and flux
>>clinging in vertigo and fear
>>to this space-shelf, peering
>>through the speeding dark
>>daring a look;

but the mirror is grained with age
and we can only see
>narrowly
>>through a veiling cloud
>>the eye no one can fully meet
>>without turning to vapor

                                  or cinder.
Yet it is not all:
what the archaic skull, the massive jaw spell
is not all.
          In the carved rotting flesh
          in the grin of the Halloween fruit
          a candle is lit;
          rainbow-fish dance in the stream;
          generations of studious bees
          replenish the hexagons of wax.
People greet each other, touch, kiss
and a bird sings, alive in the bush
brighter, more precious
                    than limp feathers
                    in a squeezing hand.

We sit
      by the water
      by the fire
      by the tree
watching the ropes of light descending
          knot upon blazing knot
          from autumn skies
as the world around us explodes
          scattering perfume and seed.
We know, yes,
              you are coming
              on the ladder of two thousand years
each instant a step that brings you nearer
              and more real than grape or bread.
Lord
      look upon your people
          the parade of the living
          the cortege of the dead.
Does your world turn into froth
does your people merge with the soil

to enrich the dandelion and the clover?
The safety latch is broken;
>   dark roots slither
>   through cracks in the floor;
>   the roof leaks, the cupboard is bare
>   save for this crust we offer
>   save for this cup into which we are poured
>   with a measure of watered wine.

❊   ❊   ❊

> — *Lift up your hearts.*
>   — *We lift them up to the Lord.*

Red
>   pinned to a centerfold of flesh
the heart speaks
>   in staccato
>   in hot flashes of blood:
a time machine ticking off minutes
>   years;
a metronome
>   counting the beat.
What can we lift?
What spark can we pluck
>   from the cockscomb
>   in the breast?
Scattered atoms from broken worlds
fly across the remote path;
ashes of old campfires mingle with the soil;
like water
>   the ages of man seep
>   through the cracked stones.
But we say love   love
shaking fire-blossoms
>   in the dark
sending flames

        waltzing through the brush.
The heart grows
        intense and luminous:
we shall lift it to the sky
wear it on our sleeve and lapel:
        open poppy, day-jewel, poem
that constantly spells
        holy   holy   holy
        Lord God of power and might.
        Heaven and earth are filled with your glory.

                ✿   ✿   ✿

We come to you Father
with praise and thanksgiving
through Jesus Christ your Son we ask you
to accept and bless these gifts.

We come to you
through a wilderness of silence
our thoughts moving wordlessly
tracing a net of random trails.
It is cold in the land:
                the key of winter
                turns in the lock
                of earth, of water.
The garden which was rich with apple
        with calling bird and growing plant
        sours and freezes.
— All the chains of emotions and feelings
all the efforts to meet, touch, talk
        perish
trapped in the ice of our wintering.
We walk till we come
        to the end of the world
                end of time
                end of thought

exhausted dumb creatures
lost in the confusion of tongues.
What language shall we speak?
What word shall be the diamond
      to cut the glass, break the ice
      release the flow of life?
God
      you are
          everywhere   anywhere   nowhere
          to be seen.
Out of the chambers and streets
      of many lives, of many years
we come
      preciously holding what we saved:
a little wheel of bread
image of the endless circling of our hungers;
a splash of wine
in a cup where the sun of all our thirsts
trembles and shines....

❁   ❁   ❁

— Take and eat: this is my body.

He makes the time
          improvises the place:
he speaks himself
          into earth
             water
             air
             fire.
Under nail and thorn
under rod and spear
they scream
      the four elements of his mastering.
In its cave, the heart weeps
not tears but healing fluids

bright semen, seeds of worlds to be.
Do we know the tidings, see
the final shape of all that fluctuates
between birth and death?
Forms in fusion, chanced words
become safe and solid vehicles
carriers of love.

Look at the rose-real
            real rose blooming marvelously
            taking space
            in the narrow realness of our gazing.
Enclosed
        we are enclosed
        having no more than the eye
        to see, missing
        what most really appears
        beyond our sight.
He marks the time
        improvises the place
        speaks himself alive
        in a flake of bread.

— *Take and drink: this is my blood.*

We die of thirst by the sea-mouth
            — Oh, bitter water —
We die of thirst by the streams and waterfalls
            — Oh, beautiful water-lights
            silver and amber rings
            locked circles in which we drown —
Our private human paths twist
like ropes through stubble fields
and the dust rises, the tree sleeps
without greening.
Our human words turn
            always at the same angle

      — not knowing how
      not knowing why —
      return to the same stillness.
But he breaks the silence
his voice cutting clear through
    the countries of the past
    a stream flowing through the rock
    in time
        out of time
flooding the depth of our need.
        — Oh, sweet and saving rain
        that soaks the root of our desire
        wakes the dormant seeds
        of the holy garden of Eden —

— Let us proclaim the mystery of faith:
    Christ has died
    Christ is risen
    Christ will come again.

The pages of history curl
    in the fire we kindle from age to age:
what taste of death teases the mind
that we stare and cannot turn
from the burning past
from the spreading stain of blood?
On the pages of history
    the script is blurred
but we decipher your name
               CHRISTOS
as our finger follows
the shape of each wound.
  — Rose-red, the poem bleeds
drop by dazzling drop —
You died, we hear the news
over the radio, see your face
on the screen of a thousand wars

— Hiroshima   Babi-Yar   Mylai —
Gunned down, hung, atomized, you return
dying over and again, descending
deeper and deeper into the spiral of death
each time a young man falls
each time a woman screams
as the child in her arms turns to stone.
With you we are locked in the shell
nested in the clay-egg, waiting
for the tremor and the touch
to break the walls.
What is heard in the mind, the cry
that dips and rises with every lilt of air
the voice muffled through layers of time
grows imperative, moans and labors.
The word we strive to utter
          and cannot speak
                              LOGOS
beginning and end of all speech
bursts forth, spills
                    sunseeds   moon-sap   stars
substantiating the shadows
that flicker on the cave's walls.
From the dark root of ourselves
we are lifted on delicate stems
released into daylight.
                              CHRIST
in the aurora   the crystal   the ray
of your coming
          we rise
and begin infinitely to say YES.

✣   ✣   ✣

Amen   Amen   Amen

Under our steps
            pebbles shine
wet with moonlight.
The garden path leads deep
into a night so baffling
            the mind hesitates and slackens:
to follow shall we come to a place
where crows are hunched
            over a half-finished meal
            over raw meat and dripping hide?
Shall we discover cruelty
our own body under their claws
the talon of death digging our skull?
We know:
            the pale glow of morning
            wakes new sorrows, shakes the downy nest
            where soft dreams were hatching.
We know:
            all that is nurtured and fed
            falls in time like stones in a well
            from which no echo does arise.
We are children of air   of water
our hair smells of tangled grass
                        of earth
our mouth is flooded
                        with all the juices
of plants   barks   leaves.
Generation upon generation of hunters
sleep in our bones;
            the light is dim
the eye of the cave glares at our back
our days dangle like spider threads
from stars millions of miles away.
But we live

not of memory but of life;
we speak
    and our words move upward
like columns we carve and lift
to shape porticos   houses   temples.
We are moved to say
            our Father in heaven.
No need to imagine altitude
a place beyond the airways
further than moon-waves and star.
No need to weave
        with strings of words
a cat's cradle
        to rock the thought of you.
You are
    here   now
        a singular rhythm
that commands the movements of heart, of breath.
Wake us:
    we lie wrapped
    in sheets of white stillness;
wake us
    to the knowledge of your name
that we may see how it is spelled
in each dust mote, each eyelash
in reflections   patterns   designs
of each random moment.
Your kingdom begins
            here   now
in these bones   this flesh
these scooping palms
        dipped in the stream of life.
How long, how long ago did you walk
in the first garden, your words seeding
the weather, falling
            into fish-form

                    bird-shape, the history of man?
Let us grow
      out of the narrowing way.
The blind instant squeezed by grasping hands
bleeds; the latex of time sticks
to the fingers, remains unshaped:
loss   loss   impermanence
                    a will as loose as water.
What can rise
          from nebulae of wishes?
Let us enter the kingdom: from brokenness
cinders, potsherds of the past
let us build a new house
            a spaciousness of love
strong stairs for our weighted steps.
Give us what we need
              and help us care
              for what we hold
this wounded living earth
torn under our heels.
In the hungry land we eat
what falls from the table, fighting
for crumbs with little dogs of pain:
their needle-teeth pierce
              the skin of our days.
Shall we survive the oil slick
the red haze, the grief carried
              by empty wombs?
Forgive us our lapses!
        Warm around our shoulders
      is the wool of our ease.
Our eyes are hard coals
          darkly
                  remotely burning
          in deep sockets of fear.
They look inward

to their own phantoms
hide in caves
       sealed against the sight
       of dripping wax, of melting life.
Our ears are plugged
       against the cry that breaks
the shell in which we sleep
softly curled upon our harsh questions
our dreamy whisperings.
Deliver us from evil
       cut the coils of confusion
       the choking noose of lust
       the net in which, caught and thrashing
       we spend our meager strength.
Drive away
    basilisks and serpents:
scaly slithering beasts, they haunt
our private land, live concealed
in the maze of our skull.
Deliver us from the last illusion
when, held to the lips,
       the unclouded mirror reflects
       a face gone still and cold.
Let us know: death does not scatter.
With a broom of steel
       it sweeps through all paths
       city streets   back lots   country lanes.
The settling dust descends
       speckles our bread
       films the poured milk.
We eat, we drink:
       death moves in our blood
       breeds in the hollows of our mind.
Father
    speak your Christ-word among us
    wash our eyes at the fount of his wisdom

that we may see
        through the glass now dark and stained
        by the smoke of our human fires:
        they rage uncontained from night to night
        giving but little heat
        hardly a cupful of glitter.
Let us know: death unravels the cloak
        we now wear thin and tattered.
            Free
        we cry out, born beyond the hood
            of sky   of smoke
        to a vastness we cannot imagine
        of light, of ever-rising light.

                    ❊   ❊   ❊

— The peace of the Lord be with you
wherever you are
        wherever people meet
station   street-corner   beach.
They lie side by side
        but cannot touch;
they walk together
        hip against hip
        but cannot merge.
Man without wife, without daughter
mother without son, woman without lover
they struggle to read
        in moon-tides
        in water-rings
direction   mysterious command   order
to go on living.
        Trees give no sign
their trembling delivers no clue.
Whatever speaks in the sky
        — great ram   fish
        scorpio   bull —

hangs on air, shines without magic.
The peace of the Lord reaches
             through the latticed door
             breaks the lock of the room
where people wait and wonder:
what if the flame of the red rose
burns out, falls without seed?
What if the wall curves into a tower
a circle of eternal illusion?
Bombs   knives   a long and naked blade
a woman tied   a mangled child.
                  Christ
the waves of pain beat
             upon your ankles.

                  ✵   ✵   ✵

Communion Rite

Nightly
        by moon-rise, lamplight
O darlings, helpless in the dark
        keep time
        keep watch;
the arm of the metronome swings
        back and forth
        slicing space, counting;
the music soars, thins
             into pinpoints of sounds;
the moment turns, slides
             from past to present,
             burns
             in lamps
             in modest flames that leap
             from paper-curls, applewood

                    pine cones set
                    upon the stony hearth.
O darlings passing
          dark
                    through the light
          shedding garment, dream, becoming
          smoke that moves upward
          with the breath of ashes
          with the last palpitation of the day.
Pray
          for the nail of light to shine
          piercingly in your soul,
          for the comb of light to change
          the tangle of life
          into silken strands,
O darlings
          moving dark
                    into the light
          of many houses, many places
          take this radiant body:
          the Dancer and the dance are one
          settled without shadow
          on the common ground.
Perception   emotion   touch
the flesh of language stretched
over dry bones of thoughts
cannot dress his unimaginable coming.
The mind splits, the inner eye
suddenly sees the fabulous truth:
at the left   at the right   here   there
in pebble   leaf-rot   in the single clipped hair
in water-knots   in weeds
                    HE IS
                    active verb
                    respiration that surges
                    ever-fresh

in the universal lung
in the breast of the living.

— This is my body:
            take and eat —

Knowledge hard to hold
            of illimitable form
            coming close
                        soundless
                        faceless
            continually ongoing
            food to eat
            manna from outer distance
wine-sea to drink
            out of the tilted cosmic bowl.
Hunger silently screams
            — gaping mouths, hearts cut open
            by the knife of need
            to be filled, to be healed —
Life patched sewed up   cleaned
and
            upon the brow
                        a coolness of wind
                        the freshest breeze
                        the breath of God.

— Go in peace! —

Seen once
            through a chink of glass
                        of time
            beyond winter's frozen words
seen once:
            great God, light
            forever stabbing
            the one part of the brain

that moonly rests in night-dust;
God
    seen beyond/within:
        the stick's fibers peeled back
        the seed quartered, the atom split;

where?
    Voice calling from the grass-harps
    hand of mist and air upon the face
    light to which the sun is shade?

— Go in peace!

                SEEK!

A Garland of Straw

Why Do You Weep?

*F*eel the arrangement of your bones
     the structure of your hand
        splayed open
           into five separate fingers.
What they touch:
     small things
     — of metal, cloth or wood —
     smoldering, unknown to you
        in the great electric wave
           the dance of atoms.
See what is carved in the rock
     upland where water falls
     into water, slicing the stone
        with a single liquid thread.
Ancient is your memory:
unknown to you, it travels back
        to the "O" of origin, the moist cave
        the roundness of the womb.

Since the beginning
I speak to you
I am the Word
     of your time
     of your name
     of your tribe and speech.
The figures I trace
     — turning wheels, coils
     of suns and moons —
let them spin and sparkle
     in your blood.
Why do you weep?

Why do you hop on one leg
        pretending you are a crippled bird
                looking for pity?
Hear the marvelous sounds:
        your heart trembling in its cage
        your life shouting life
                through the pores of your skin.
Hear the cadence I tap
        on the drum of your wrist.
You are made to catch the rhythm
        to know you are danced alive
        in the Fire from which no ashes fall:
"I am that Fire"
        says the Lord.

Not Enough

"The poor are going to feed in my pastures, and beggars rest in safety." (Isaiah 14:30)

I do not know how to begin:
I am tired, the threads are tangled
    the frame is warped and worn.
I look for a tool
    a needle of sharp knowledge
to piece words together
      into an all-American quilt
        — the pattern, of wheels and rings
          of great eagles spiraling forever
          over corn-yellow fields.

Nothing seems enough!
Why is it that I always wish
    for more than the eye can hold?
The blue wash of the sky
the pleased look in the mirror
    — not enough, not enough!
The spirit hungers, roams
    seeks farther abroad
for something essential to eat:
    muscles and flesh
    and cracking bones of truth.

How could I lie down in winter
    warm in a warm room
the quilt of language pulled over my head
muffling the sound of hurried steps:
    all those people
      cold, starved, looking for food?
Beauty is
    earth

fire
        water
            and air
    transmuted into bread
        through long and painful toiling.
Lord, give me the power to be spent
        in the grinding and the shaping
        only of such words
        as will feed the multitude!

World News

"O Lord, in distress they sought thee, they poured out a prayer when thy chastening was upon them." (Isaiah 26:16)

We are all standing in the dark
    letter-carriers, messengers
sent across mountain paths
    to deliver the morning news;

      ASIA is drowning
    its thousand hands slipping down
      scraping the hulls of wrecked boats
    its thousand mouths bitterly rinsed
    its words turning to salt!

We come to speak about an angry woman
    AFRICA!
Pure black, her body stripped
she rises from her shores
    dripping diamonds and blood.
Muttering like drunken men
we hand out photographs of
    AMERICA:
    sheets printed with replicas
    of people translated into a million dots
      inked on the pages of leaflets and memos.

We are not safe on this planet
this mudball rolling
in a dust of dead stars.
Like pocket-mirrors held to the sun
we burn with many lights
    send signals of ice and fire
      to other spheres.
We ask for entry

our skins blistered
       our minds breaking out in flames
we stand in the dark by the last door
pleading:

"Open to us, Lord:
we bring you the morning news!
We are in danger from hunger and thirst
       from basilisks and dragons.
The real and the unreal mingle
       flow into a single question
— and how are we to learn
       and how are we to know?
We want only simple things:
       a square of space, time enough
       to spell ourselves clear against the dark.
We want to hold on to common things
              bread, doorknob, bed frame.
Lord, we can live this life
if you give us what we need:
       more than gravity, grace
              to grip the earth
              to stay on!

Bread to the Hungry

"If you do away with the yoke, the clenched fist, the wicked word; if you give your bread to the hungry and relief to the oppressed your light will rise in the darkness and your shadows will become like noon." (Isaiah 58:10)

In the grey hour of the evening
    clutching plate and fork
we get ready to eat.
What are these shadows
    clustered by the window?
What is the muffled sound
    outside, by the flame of the gladioli?
Leathery claws grip the windowsill
small shriveled faces peer through the screen.

By the window, at dusk
    the poor of the world assemble.
They are very old
    even the children
    even the little girls
        with eyes like brown moths.
They carry wooden bowls
    of ancient shape;
they do not speak.
Theirs is a country of eternal heat
    of sand lifted like smoke
        by desert winds.

If you give bread to the hungry....

Sugared loaves are stacked
    on shelves and table-tops.
We slice them thickly
    toast them under controlled heat
    set our jaws to the crust.

We are giants sitting on mountain tops
        toying with our food; we eat at leisure
        chewing great chunks of space
        biting a crescent off the moon
                — its texture white and soft
                made of the finest milled flour.
With strong squared teeth
        we grind acres of wheat
        cut through the sweet glaze
        the honey of the world.
Outside
        these ghosts
        these silent bony people
                stare at us, banging their empty bowls
                hard against the walls.

If you give bread to the hungry....

We must hurry:
        no time left
                soon
        no life left in these souring bodies
        no light left in our darkening souls.
Come out of the desert
        brothers, sisters
sit with us in the open
        on the brilliant green grass
and let us share this bread:
        the loaves multiplied by love
        under caring outstretched hands.

In the Dark We Drink

"Then deep from the earth you shall speak, from low in the dust your words shall come." (Isaiah 19:4)

We cannot move back:
 the road is blocked
  on which we traveled
  light and easy
  on the track of certitudes.
If we look over our shoulder
we see, at odd angles of time
  women's smiles locked in photographs
  hands held in mid-air
   forever waving good-byes.
Distantly, voices hail us
  the sound diffused, obstructed
  hardly reached this present space
  we fill with new words, new shapes.
Yesterday, we could pluck knowledge
  a childish flower
  a blue morning-glory
   planted by the fence
    on the sunny side of the mind.
Now, we crawl through the underground
  our miner's lamp pulsing with heat
   clamped to our forehead.
We choke on black dust;
our eyes grow enormous, strain
  to perceive the golden fleck
   embedded in the face of the rock.
Sometimes we hear water
  dripping from the stone
  icy-cold, speaking
  fresh syllables, almost a song.
We cup our hands:
  in the dark, we drink.

Be at Rest

"Fear not, for I have redeemed you. I have called you by name, you are mine." (Isaiah 43:1)

Your body against mine
        says the Lord.
I feel its quivering substance
        its soft shapeless mass
displacing itself, moving away
        a grain at a time
        a year at a time
pulling away from me.
Why are you restless?
You wear your eyes hooded
        like the desert snake;
the words you speak crackle
        dry and hot.
What do you fear?

How astounded you were
        in the beginning
        in the first wet millennium:
you did not know my name
        only the nudge of my will
        stirring your life.

I know the stories you invent
        your betrayals, your lies.
I know your silence
        how silently you approach
        hoping I would not notice
        what you are about to do:
hammer me still, drive the nail
        into the raw nerve of my speech

kill what you cannot tame
        and shape to your wishing.

You cannot escape:
at your right and at your left
        before you and beyond
it is I, the Lord, this strange element
        in which you are caught
                thrashing about
                gasping for breath
                drowning.
The islands of your hands
remain afloat while you submerge
        sink like a stone within my depths.
Stone-flesh
your weight pressed against mine
        tears me open.
Be still:
my blood is threading itself
        spinning its red filaments
                around your limbs.
Child
you cannot move away:
you are the chrysalis in my silk
        the slow-waking creature
                waiting for the ultimate transport
                        for wing-power and wind.
Child
        your body against mine:
let it rest
        not to descend
                blind, unfeeling into death
        but to rise
                conscious of the light
        to complete your history
                reach your final form.

Passiontide

"And the crowds were appalled on seeing him; so disfigured did he look that he seemed no longer human; so will the crowds be astonished at him and kings stand speechless before him; for they shall see something never told and witness something never heard before." (Isaiah 53:14-15)

*L*ook
   who is coming down the road
      like nothing heard before
      like nothing we can understand:
         that poor shirtless man
         not a cent, not a friend to his name
         dragged by soldiers
         pushed to his death
         by the crowd!
It cannot be
   God cannot be an actual fact
   a statistic, a murdered man
   hanging on crossed posts!

In the past, we lived
   with that figure on a throne
      old Father Time, holding the hourglass
      through which passively we flowed.
From the sun, we took a little fuel;
from the moon, silver words, rhymes
   to rock us to sleep.

Now we must look
   deeper than we know.
Like nothing seen before
   God is a dead Jew
      his body packed with myrrh
      his wounds smeared with oil.
Like nothing we can understand

he wakes to life
rises lighter than light
through dark breaking gates.
The hourglass shatters:
no longer are we jammed together
pressed down through death's funnel
like coarse cold sand.
We are free
move at a changed pace
and begin anew!

*News of the World
in Fifteen Stations*

Jesus Meets His Mother

*D*on't say it was easy
        no matter the star
        no matter the brooms of light
            sweeping hilltops in the dark:
birth is bloody, a mess
        of fluid and torn flesh.
Women know, they who open their legs
        to push the child into a net of time.
It was not sweet
        yet if ever there was sweetness on earth
        it was that first meeting, first sight
            in the rank straw of centuries.
He was wrapped, a small packet of skin
        wrapped round and round, swaddled
            in soft hand-woven cloth.

On a loom of sorrow
        their lives, mother and son
        stretched out.

           ✻   ✻   ✻

Ark of the Covenant
        Tower of Ivory
            House of Gold
                Mystical Rose:
her names shine with reflected light
        silver threads pulled
            through the dull fabric of the world.
Lady of the Garden
        Lady of the Moon
she alone without hunger

she alone without thirst
complete in her own word.
Lady, pray for those who tend fire
feeding oil to lamps, throwing sticks
to the flames under the cooking pots.
Autumn, fat with fruit
turns into rib-showing winter;
centuries tumble one after the other
collapse in tired heaps;
rags, bones, paper hats
fuel the fire women feed
steadily with everlasting gestures
in everlasting toil.

❋   ❋   ❋

Pray for those who do not see
who cannot hear the humming bees
at work in meadows of affliction
in shrouded fields of despair.
Pray
for those bearing the mark
of servitude in factory, in orchard
in shiphold and coal-mine:
the whip invisible
the branding iron concealed
yet applied again and again
to hunched sagging backs.
Pray
for all who are afraid
of the shady side of the road
sound of boot on gravel
knock in the middle of the night.
Pray
for us who fear death
by knife, by rope, by bitter brew

death disguised as a hag
        offering bright apples
death riding through the mind
        a faceless stranger
            a hunter looking for meat.

Pray
for those who gather crumb and rind
        thankful for one cabbage leaf
        for one grain of rice.
for those who collect
        the loose change of words:
hear how they jingle
        in the pockets of preachers
        in the beggar-bowls of poets.
Anoint these hands
        that mend and bind and glue
            broken pieces, shattered lives.
Pray for us now
        and at the hour of our death.

Jesus Dies on the Cross

"Jung comments that in some traditions the cross is a symbol of fire and of the suffering of existence and that this may be due to the fact that the two arms were associated with the kindling sticks which primitive people rubbed together to produce fire and which they thought of as masculine/feminine."

*B*ones of ice
       bluish face veiled by sorrow
back straining against brute force
       against the dicta of thrones
       powers and dominations:
he dies
       beaten, shot, gassed
       hung, atomized
       into a no-where of winter.

"Five, six, pick up sticks"
       chant the freezing children;
       twigs are rubbed together:
in the crossing of the wood
       the rose of fire quickens.

Drawn to flame and light
       we enter the space where he burns
bright tiger-Christ
       in forests too dark for sight
       in caves where hunters assemble.
What are we doing?
       We sit, stand, move about
discuss the weather, plan
       birthdays, weddings, vacations.
Under huge crystal icicles
       Mozart plays a little night music:
exquisite sound, rapture

while outside the gate
the condemned dies:
    King of the Jews among the rubble.

The earth shakes
    the charnel-house breaks open
    releases a rank odor
centuries of corpses
    millennia of decay.

Terror lifts its hooded head
    looks us in the eye.
Born to die: why this riddle?
    Where on earth do they fly
    these few years we count
    as arrows in a soon-empty quiver?

Often, in gladness, we say, "Here we are!"
    but tomorrow we lose the place
    become wanderers
    beyond the cherished allotted tract:
    home is where we are not.

In the end, all the familiar voices
    flute, oboe, rain and wind
    the swish of petals, leaves and wings
    all soothing words and calming songs
    merge into one inaudible whisper.

He dies, we die with him.
Here, there, now and then
    the body of the world
        — feminine/masculine
        mother/father bound —
    hangs by threads of fire
        in the sweep and the roar of time
            compressed around its burning center.

Jesus Is Risen

Stretched-out
>   his body rests on the seven continents
>   his limbs touch the poles, north and south
>   his heart at the center of the city
>>   sleeps amidst the congress of the dead.

"Before Abraham was, I AM."

His voice drills through the rock
>   shatters the winter-locked room.
He comes forth
>   first-born of the morning
to the lips and breasts of the earth
>   — his beloved —
nursing and being nursed
>   in newly-found eternity of flesh.
"His left hand is under my head
>   and his right hand embraces me."

Something no one teaches
>   no one mentions to us:
the conscious sudden flash
>   the jubilant "I am":
first whiff of selfhood
>   of life filling our nostrils
with the scent of apple-blossom
>   on a lonely lane of childhood.
Something no one dares to say:
>   — giant stones block the way
>   seal the threshold
>   obscure the gate to the wedding hall —
we fear the body
>   its opulence and light

more than death, we fear life
    the radiance in the foliage hidden:
the eyes, the hair, the mouth
    the unwavering hand yanking the threads
      unraveling the shroud.

Within the chrysalis
    the creature stirs
tears the walls of its chamber
    unfolds the drapery of its wings
— small, delicate, yet multiplied
    thousand upon thousand
angel-butterflies take flight
    out of his hands, out of his wounds.

In the reflection of his face
    leaves unroll their amazing substance
    proclaim the green reign of his will.
Milky sap shoots into fibrous stems
    extends the branching into flower and seed.
Rain in brilliant strands streams
    through his fingers and he says;

"Drink, beloved ones, drink of these worlds
    that irrigate the longing of the race;
with quick and steady tongue, lap
    the water that I am
    gathered in the cup that I am.
Drink: your endless thirst
    shall be endlessly slaked."

"I come into my garden
    my sister, my bride
I gather my myrrh and my balsam
    I eat my honey and my honeycomb
    I drink my wine and my milk.
Eat, beloved, drink;
    drink deep, beloved."

Why do we resist, prefer
	our underground lodgings
	our dry roots, our empty dishes?
It is hard to crawl
	out of constricting shapes
to shed membrane, integument
	our animal skin, our vegetal cloak.
It is hard to be born to our full selves
	to reach full size and form.

Out of shade and shadow
	God, Father/Mother/Midwife
pulls us as we whimper
	through the birthing door.
And here we are, here we become
	words of a new language
	steps of a new dance
spiraling in the ascending mode
	with the Sun/Christ.
From dark nests
	from cells and caves
from depths of turbulence and pain
	we rise
and find ourselves oriented
	moving, full-fleshed, full-faced
	into the flaming light.

❊   ❊   ❊

"After that I saw a huge number, impossible to count, of people from
every nation, race, tribe and language; they were standing in front of
the throne and in front of the Lamb, dressed in white robes and hold-
ing palms in their hands. They shouted aloud: 'Victory to our God who
sits on the throne and to the Lamb.' And all the angels who were stand-
ing in a circle round the throne surrounding the elders and the four
animals, prostrated themselves before the throne and touched the
ground with their foreheads, worshipping God with these words:
'Amen! Praise and glory and wisdom and thanksgiving and honor and
strength and power to God forever and ever!'" AMEN

A Passion Play

Jesus Washes Peter's Feet

He washes Peter's feet, puts on his outer garment, and returns to the table.

Jesus (*to Peter*):
   Do you understand what I have done?
   Do you see what is coming
   converging from all directions upon you —
   day after day, people traveling
   through the cloud-dusts of time?
   They carry suitcases of trouble
   packs of assorted folly
   bedrolls feathered with lies.
   They keep coming, Peter
   hundreds of centuries from now
   the same harlequins, powdered
   wigged, body-painted, with smiles
   slashed into their flesh like wounds.
   They shiver with shame, curse
   spit in your face, in your great rock-face
   pockmarked, pitted by age-long rains.
   A miserable yet glorious lot
   thieving, whoring, tumbling helter-skelter
   twenty thousand years down the roads
   on crutches, in rags: my people, Peter
   my honey from the buzzing hive
   my gift to you. You will stand
   rooted in this place, chained to this washing:
   the water that now cleans you
   will pearl in your hands, healing
   opening sealed eyes to see
   not shells of ruined worlds
   not broken systems and rusted machines
   but the eternal man rising, one among many
   one for all, out of the primal mud
   out of the stone.

Act III

Jesus (*to the weeping women*):
Women of Jerusalem
do not weep over me:
but if tears must fall, let them flow
over yourselves, over your children.
And if you must wail, let your voices
rise beyond this hour and break a passage
through the hard stone of time.
I mourn with you, my sisters:
hate fans the fire under the cauldron
where you simmer. Why, queens of sorrow
does your hair blaze under flaming crowns?
From age to age
why is guilt pressed upon your souls?
Crush the myrrh, prepare the linen
store the ointment for your distant children.
The desert, the rock-pile, the lime-pit
this is where you keep house, my sisters!
With you I mourn, with you I am sent
by cattle-car to sealed rooms
deep into a smoky darkness.
My sisters, in my dying I sing Kaddish with you.
I am not a God of nowhere, but Myriam's son;
my roots stand firm in your soil, Israel!
Who is killing me? A few Romans
a handful of Jews? Here and now, yes;
but my death grows elsewhere, hangs
in a thousand evil trees. The hands
that kill hold the club, aim the gun
drop the bomb; the eyes that hunt me
glow in dark forests of time; I die
in all places of terror, at all hours
       — Rome, Constantinople, Auschwitz
       Hiroshima, Babi-Yar, Mylai —

names are tattooed on my flesh
numbers are carved in my wrists
while the world writes its history
with the iron alphabet of war.
    Weep, daughters of Jerusalem: I weep with
you
        for if they slash the green wood
        what shall they do to dry branches?

Readings: A Book of Hours

Matins

BLACK
     bitter night.
The only tools, modest clubs
     needles of bone pulling leather strips
     through the gap of millennia.
Light, uninvented, sleeps
     in cloud and flintstone.

        "A":

Alpha of consciousness
Adam standing up
     — his fur shed
     brilliantly naked —
     crosses the boundaries
     filters through time's slits and cracks
     in a paradise of awakening.

What signs?
     The carved rock, the bloody gut
     prophecies of the masked dancer:
he runs here in the street
     climbs stairs
     crashes through the door
     falls through layers of sleep.
What moves behind his eyelids?
landscape of flood, disaster, fire
juxtaposition of water and flame
animals swimming
     pale and magical
        in his head.
In the beginning
     darkly

the child sucks its thumb, holds
    the secret of the world
    the amazing numbering of the stars:
sight, touch, the power to name
    to rage, weep, love.
Eternal, enchanting, life moves
    head-first
through the great chambers of the world
towards the likeness of man.
Shall the womb be scraped
    language killed
    the voice clipped
        before the first sound can rise
        and become song?

Night hangs at the window
    a square of black silk
    drawn over the face, hiding all
    but the living eyes.
On the outer side:
    movement in the grass
    hunger of lions
    thirst of rasping tongues
        coming to the garden pool.
On the inner side
    within the soul's passages
    ancient roots work their way
    through mortar and stone
— a greening stem
a great hook of knowledge
    pierces the mind.
Revived, delivered
    into the words of our waking
what do we say
    but contradicted good-mornings
what do we show

but contractions of fingers
over knobs of sleep?

Lord
    open the shutters of time
        the gateway of speech.
When we leave the night's cave
shall we remember the dream-house
    dream-city through which we passed
    counting birthdays, counting death
    by fire, flood, tormented wishing?
What was handed to us
    through dark vaporous doors?
What password, skill, sign
    from what outreaching past?

Lord
    see these cold words change
    from deep to pale color
    as the future begins to shine
    in brilliant prophecies:
a power, bright and blowing
    shakes the crown of flowering trees;
stars leave us, the moon turns away
    to lift other seas.

Lord
    we come
        into the dailiness
        of bread, room, street.

Bless us
    as the bird of dawn sends
    to our waking brain
    a first needle of sound.

Prime

From the turned page
    in the book of creation
words fatten into substantial forms:
let there be light!
And light comes to the hand
    the aluminum roof, the milk
    in the glass pitcher on the table.
In the tree
    green with life before time
    the bird of the first stanza
    begins to sing:
    music shapes the world
    feathers house the new day.
Structured bodies in structured rooms:
    bone answers beam
    eye measures the distance.
Shall we walk on the penciled line
    holding what we own
    in precise equilibrium
or shall each moment be invention
    a fleshing act:
        words over the spine of thoughts
        skin over rushing blood
        color coating common facts
        violet for sorrow
        red for love?
On the huge canvas
    the aurora becomes an imperative
    a power forcing out of earth and wood
    a world of resonance, an art
    hatched whole and living.
Water washes over us
    a loose, flickering thing

rising from sacred deep caves
to enfold, to cling, to fit us
skin-tight in silver chill.
We live by association
by the curve and turn of images:
where has it dripped away
the time when good-morning held
the roundness of a child waking
to oatmeal and sea-sounds
— water-bells of the waves
gong in the heart of the shell?
The lost garden is a pinpoint on the map:
where are the flamingos and the peacocks
hand-fed tigers and monkeys?
Eve, that odd, unremembering woman
comes to the breakfast table
offering
with coffee
an apple half-eaten.

Lord
the summer crackles underfoot.
The winter to follow
will be stone, hard against the knuckles.

Lord
does the subway mouth lead
to your underground
to the gold vein of your love
the sapphire of your speech?
Or shall it bring us dead-center
in the wrong of hellish pain
— throat slit, pockets picked clean of hope?

Lord
bless this day
for you, beyond counting;

for us, a small uncertain measure
a spoon dipped in a protean sea.
Yet, how can this be
that we are mad with the thrill
of seeing the sun lit:
fire restored
lamp set high, set firmly in the mind
revealing durations, epochs
all ages and norms of man?
Seeing is believing:
Lord, we know!

Lauds

*F*orty days and forty nights
    through the desert:
we walk from past to future
    shedding the fleece of old
    leaving the meat stewing
        in the clay pots of Egypt;
    moving where
        — quails in the wind
        corn-flakes in the morning —
    where the opening sea
        the cloud
            the fire-pillar
                show the way.
Daylight falls still in the room
    where bed, chair, glass
    the rose bleeding on the table
    settle in solid utterances.
We enter the fold of garments
    the hollowness of sleeves
adjust over eye and mouth
    the pigments of the ceremonial mask.
Groomed and shod, we are ready
    to pass through an imagined door
    to enter a new world.

Something moves through the cloud
    a voice moves alive
    moves life into flesh
        into man, woman
        into the sparrow's throat
        and the seed's core.
Shall we drive on
    past these rocks shaped

by fingers of sand
or choose a single stone, altar
        to offer aromatic wood, a handful of fire?
We come
        with disconnected words:
            "Light"
                we say;
                    "Lord"
                        we say
        offering the crackling manna
        pouring the milk of dreams
        into the breakfast bowl.
The desert has sifted its crystals
        into our blood: we carry these particles
                silence, solitude, wild wishing
        in the ache of our soul.

Lord
        in the country of the morning
we row the sandy rivers
        choking on dust and smoke.
The walls
        — of animal skins
        stretched on crossed poles —
        can be folded, carried
        a thousand miles against the wind.
Memories glimmer
        jingle like coins
        in our pocket.
We breathe time
        in and out
stretch our arms
        like branches to the sun.

Lord
        yes, we praise thee!

150

Terce

*D*ark-hearted with seeds
        sunflowers line the garden path.
  Yes, we have seen the pleasant house:
        pears on the windowsill
        coffee on the table
        books, green plants, a new fire
            growing under bundled twigs.

Lord
        can we break the crust of this day
        can we lift the cup, drink this hour
            before it turns brackish and brown
            seeps away through the cracking glaze?
Over and over, we twined
        one moment to the next
our hands steady
        trying for a pattern never held before.
Twisted in the love-knot of your making
hidden in the form of your secret
        we are
            Lord
            naked only in your sight.
Through all these rooms
      — small and smoked
      mere chinks in the face of the rock —
we move bone to bone
      breast to breast
      dressed in each other's speech
      in the silk of our mutual giving.

Lord
      we have thieved:
      in the ancient distance

apple of succulence
first knowing of misuse
            of disconnection
sweet morning fruit
golden intelligence flashing
the fortune of its thoughts:
("*Our* knowledge," we say
    adding another coin
    to the careless heap.)

Behind us:
    glitter, mortality, pain!
Before us:
    glitter, mortality, pain!
Yet, so many years in the finding
    this one clear space
    this place where planets and pebbles
            animals, flowers, men
    mesh in the convergence of your sight!

We speak
    we are spoken.
We call
    we are called
and the voice never fails
but increases
changes from one intensity to another
forming new sounds:
        "O"
of wonder, of openness
gold disk, ornament of winter
gate to let in
        O your Sun!

Sext

*E*arth eroded, stones shifting
   tigers nearly extinct
      and time?
Time waterfalls away from us.
In the melting noon
     all things drop
     ripe and open
     fruits of the half-way
     to be eaten on the road
     before the whistle blows.
Where are we?
      Is the day a coil around us
        a locking circle?
Or is it set deep in an ancient wall
a window looking out
     towards pastures
        beribboned children
          legions of angels?

O world of common sight
     of sweat and cry, argument and tension
     penumbra that calls light:
here we are
     home in the green shade of the maple
     patterning the dust with our weight
     pecking with the sparrows
       the crumbs of the past.
We came from buried cities
     from the pits where bones are gathered
     wing-bones, antlers, tail-rings and tusks;
we came from the formlessness of water
     from the curve and twist of millennia
       the bending of the bow, the arrow flying....

We came together, many-voiced
        and the stories we tell
            recounted from age to age
        hang in the air like scrolls
            unrolling in waves of color:
        smoke-blue for all the cooled worlds
            of men and beasts and plants;
        black for the tears we shed
            through a thousand and one nights;
        green for the grass-nests
            where lovers in each other's arms
                summon the future.

Lord
        the stones of morning
        — clean-washed stoops over which
        so eagerly we tread —
        gradually darken; our shadows
        fall limp at our feet;
        we pull them
            — shadow-bodies
            shadow-worlds.
        With every step
            we haul their leaded weight.

Lord
        hidden in ourselves
        hunger screams
        thirst rakes the chalky riverbeds
            of rainless countries.
Let us find the swollen hive
        the honey-well of meaning.
We seek beyond scrawls and garbled words
        beyond the sign engraved
                on the face of the rock
the secret of the light we cut and cross:

secret of man ascending the ladder of being
    through what ruptured link
    holding what guiding thread?

Huddled against the earth's brown skin
we hear a muffled rhythm:
    beyond the proof of experience
    a remembered unknown song
        life-charged, wind-full
    lifting the smell of pitch
    from the pits
    speaking the names of dead hunters
    calling the gatherers of berries
        the pluckers of wild apples.
They come, keep coming
        in the long pause of noon
drumming words of a communal song
rubbing sticks till the flame leaps
    blue and crested
out of their distant hands
to warm the present day.

Lord
    keep us still
    as time turns on its hinges
    like a creaky door.
We cannot go on forever
    lifting the ram's horn
    to blow our screeching questions.
Hold us in soundlessness
    with mind polished
        a brass mirror in which faintly at first
        a reflection appears
        an imprint intensified
            from moment to moment
            from year to year

                        till we catch
                    without touch or sight
                the full slant of your hidden sun.
        What we see on waking
                — shape, place, the stand
            of habitual trees —
            retains its literal form:

September stains the woods: ferns are yellowing, and on the
slope where stones have marvelous dark eggplant skins, water
runs cooler, slips a silver chill through the grass. In the blur-
ring haze, the house looks brown-feathered, an old hen brood-
ing in a weedy yard. We are fingers, hands, legs at work in fast-
moving traffic — clouds in the sky, cars on the road, rotating
planets. We are silk knots of nerves set within delicate organic
shells; we are ash and limestone. Hello, good-bye! We grope
through rarefied air along tracks of vibrant energy. All of it, the
allness of all kingdoms, the juice of the universe, nectar of un-
known stars, of barely perceptible cells, flow into a cup hollowed
out of clay, sky and stone. We press it to our lips, O Lord of
the Meridian, and drink.

None

*T*iredness sets in the bone
         deep like an axe.
We have not seen the land
         promised to our tribe;
we roamed the wilderness
         leaving neither script nor track
         carrying our life, its weight
         of leather and rag
         through time's rippling waves.

Home
         is a million miles away
and what we hear, the news
         of distant battles, the cries
         of burning children
roars in our brain:
         small ghosts of supplication
         they beg through enormous spaces
         for soothing oil, a bandage
         a cup of oblivion.
It is not flesh that fills
         suit or dress or glove
but an infinite number of grains:
         sand-man   sand-woman
               we stand
blind and still
while the wind moves the world
transporting huge chunks of land
         whole cities, centuries and ages
from one dark place to another.

Smell, sight, touch:
         we long

for the brew in Egypt's pots,
     herbs, onions, lamb
the pause by the campfire
the idle talk of noon.
Who will come to us in this hour
     with lips of water
     liquid fingers
     river hair?

Lord
     we thirst!
There are no watering places
     on the moon, no pail or spoon
     to dip in the milk
     of that beautiful face.
We need no abstract terms
     cold knife of logic
     iron pincers of thoughts
     forged in hellfire.
We need no smear of moondust
     on insulated boots:
we need the earth's moisture
     the mothering ooze
     fertile womb on which to rest
     at ease and in pleasure.
We need the touch of others
     the clasping arms
     the joined hands.
We need beauty
     — she of the carved granite
     palace-figure with jeweled lid;
     she of music, poetry
     constellated with images
     resonant like bell-metal!
We need
     eyes to see

the other side of life:
what we wear close to the skin
    that rough and prickly cloth
    that wool spun with brambles
is not the whole garment.
At times, we finger the silk
    of a celestial cloak;
we hold handfuls of a fabric
    woven on a loom stretched
    from north to south, manned
    by the four servants of the wind.

GOD
    we need you!
Heal what we keep hidden
    under the thousand folds
    of our perpetual smiling:
the slashed heart
the mind grown slack
    soft under its shell
    and like the crab, burrowing
    to dark retreats.

Lord
    with a hand that is no hand
        but a diamond of shattering light
follow the contour of our pain
cut, deepen the wound
    till it becomes a door to your mercy.
Much is discomfort here:
    gritty sand mixed with manna
    the space for language
    crowded with careless words
    and hope narrowed to the sight
    of an undulating belly
    in the next oasis of the mind!

Lord
we have moved horizontally
    all over an empty land.
Now we pause to gather the black thorn
    to build a fire on the stony slab
        of this hour.
We need a sign:
Shall it be other
    than the buzzard's circling
more than the bloody stain
    of the westering sun?
It is enough
    to be
        to say
            Lord!

Vespers

*L*ong rope uncoiled
      sleeping serpent
      no flute can charm
the hour lies dark and still.
"A thousand years is like a day," says the Lord.
      Yesterday
slipping our hands
under the rock, we caught small crabs
for our supper; the place is lost:
we do not recall the stream;
our other ancient face
curtained by millennia, recedes
      in the wrinkled water.
Time drops
      from what height
      into what endless depth?
Yesterday
      our daughters shaped the world
      to the roundness of their breasts;
today
      their breath freezes
         into snow-flowers
         white roses of cold metal.
Our sons' eyes were jewels
      embers glowing in the fiery masks.
Their dreams formed a maze
      a network in which to trap
         deer and buffalo.
Today
      they do not know the earth
      as a nurse and woman.
They come home
      and life is a key in a determined slot

the turning of iron into wood
the coming into a room
where table, chair, food
are wild devouring powers.

Lord
it was given to us to dance
with the swelling of the buds
the growing of the leaves;
to invent rhythms, improvise sounds
build a temple which would hold
country, metropolis, planted field.
Now, we buy five stalks of wheat
— dried, the heads drooping —
and nail them to a wall!
Who shall buy the wind?
Who shall touch the rising moon
with rubber stamp or leather boot?
Who shall wear moon-chips
as ornaments on neck-chains?

Lord
what will happen
already happens now:
the idle fact, fattened
by numberless numbers, multiplied
added infinitely to the sum of itself:
stone upon stone, bone upon bone
dust over dust:
death
nothingness
black death!

Lord
keep the bear and the crow
away from our flesh; deliver us
from the lion's jaw.

162

In the night, they come hungering
to the bed where we lie
    folded upon ourselves
    knees up to chin
    rolling down huge mountains of sleep.
They wait among the image-trees
    dream-animals, spirit-hunters
    leaving real tracks
    inflicting real wounds.

Lord
    let us know
        even at this late hour!
The world is warm with your flesh:
water, fire, earth and air — your holy flesh
    vanquished and resurrected
    dying and ever-born
    cracking the stone open
    breaking the doors of death
        rising
    forever rising!

Lord
    this is our future:
        written in the palm's lines
        in the contour of every pebble
        in every rain-drop and cloud-shape.

We live
    not by imposed laws
    by grim deadly edicts
    but by that word which is freely spilled:
        love-seed in the sower's hand
    and the furrow wide open
        moistened by a long-ago stream.
Blessed are you
    Lord God of all creation!

Blessed are you
     for the ground of our dying!
Dust shall not sift into our sealed eyes
     shall not reach our flesh's ragged pockets.
By the door of our leaving
     you are
          setting us aswim in your saltless sea!

Complines

We read by the lamp:
> the wick slowly sucks the oil
>> feeds the flame
> even as we now draw fire
>> pluck the small lights of words
>> from the turned page.

This time
> — open space to which we come
> surfacing with root-strength —
this time shall not be lost or found
> only transcended
>> carried over and out
>> of its perpetual turn.
On the other side of the wall
> — fox, beaver, otter, bear —
they call our animal spirits
> to the moon's radiant wells.
"Come," they say, "be reborn in a dream."
But continents throb around us
> centuries stand in circles
> and history is on our mind:
>> the vast panorama of acts and laws
>> the vision rearranged a thousand times
>> by the born child, the dead man.

We have hands other than to touch
> eyes other than to see;
and the light we force
> out of oil and sticks
shines dark before the candelabra
set high on the templed stone of this hour:
seven-branched and all-knowing

it drips hot with God's wax.
The sound, a monotone of voices
    word-pellets upon the skin of silence;
the sound pulls the snake out of its coils.
The emblems on its shield
display directions: it will lead us
if we wish, to the old quarry
    the cave velvet-hung with bats
where it will grow out of itself
and around us: an iron ring
    an absolute clasp
        from which there is no breaking.

Lord
    cut the knotted syntax of the beast
    — wars, tortures, killings
    are locked in its speech:
    daily, the world gets on
    with the deadly business!

Lord
    where are delight, revelation, wonder
        the spirit of the dance
    — man dancing in and out
        of the seriousness of events
    wearing laughter
        like an ultimate cosmology:
    the twinkle of stars on his face
    the sun's blinking eye shining
        clear through his pain?

Lord of lichen and bark
    of mushroom and goldenrod
crush the shell and seed of our days
mix the pigments and press them
    bleeding-wet into the shape of your praise.

Are we more than sparrows
        more than an eyelash curve and shade?
If we must sum up
        the talk and the deed
        — Lord, this is the midnight
        of our trembling —
let our naked truth fall like a stone
speed on forever in the abyss of your mercy.

It is late: the flame, for lack of oil
        now eats the wick
        feeds on our soul's tender marrow.
When shall we know
        without lense or lamp
the reality of the real?
        We are
these bodies silver and gold
overlaid by everlasting brightness.
The great pell-mell of the hive
the buzzing sound of the swarm
conceal the master-plan
        the honey mounting in the structured cell.
Time makes a curve, draws
a hazy circle around us
tells
        — but it lies —
the alphabet we spell
the script over which we labor
dissolves equally in water or fire.
Tells
        — but it is the ghost of a truth —
the house we build day by day
is of air and spidery webbing:
rain bears down on the roof
the beams rot and through the floor
the mandragora, the man-shaped root

pushes its blind power.
When the prince of death appears
at the window, wagging a bony finger
    — Oh, the time will be ripe:
    we shall not die forever —
our hearts shall send out rays
outreaching the dark as we say

    LORD
        INTO YOUR HANDS
            WE COMMEND OUR SPIRIT.

Through the Gateless Gate

At Prayer

Somewhere
> beyond the boundaries
> of body, house, street
a space opens
> place of pilgrimage
> to which I ascend
not on hands and knees
> not crawling through mental routes
but
> flying
> with heavy flesh made light
> with arms invisibly feathered
> spread like great supportive wings.

A time of arrival, of exploration
> of becoming part of the eternal hosannah
> through which the fledgling finds
> the precise syllable of its song
and the goose returns, year after year
> to its exact locus
> by ice-fringed waters
> in the deep north.

Bad News, Good News

(Reading the newspaper in the evening.)

We thirst among dry words:
    stone — dust — straw
and more abstractly
    loss — pain — silence
    the husks of life.
Even the wind spatters our face
    with the grit of desert sand.
For a moment, we look up
    turning away from news of disasters.

In the far distances of the sky
    the whole orchestration of planets
    throbs and spins.
The moon, a tilted saucer
    pours forth its milk.
Underneath, at eye level
    not a curve, not a rounded object:
only angles and sharp corners
    only a dark hierarchy of shadows
graded from ghosted greys
    to the deepest ebony.

Daily, the world overtakes us
    its cruel details framed
        in monochrome photographs
— the violent colors blotted out
    the blood drained from the newsprint.
Everywhere, death threads itself
    through limbs, spine, heart
endlessly reading its target
    leaving behind empty places

at the communal tables
— chairs where no one sits
spaces cut by a wide swath of absences.

And God?
He crosses every threshold
enters every story
sees what is falling:
the body of the world screaming down
through circle after circle of terror.
He walks the roads of lamentations
weeps motherly tears over the slain
while in the West the piles of dry words
grow, text after text, page after page
his name ornamenting the margins
in gilded scrolled script.
Elsewhere, he bleeds to death
in a foreign street.

Who will tell
we shall not die forever?
He who was taken into the hollow rock
rises
a wild fire flowing through sinews
and articulations of life
until the whole creation begins to shimmer
becomes translucent, a house of light.

Life Rising

Passing on, going over, breaking out
    of dark muttering into speech
    of close configurations into lines
moving away from the center
    in ever-widening circles —
how can anyone suppose
    all is still in this world
    fixed into patterns forever
    echoing each other?
The whole cosmos is in motion:
    stars explode and vanish
the earth's carapace shifts
    and mutant genes travel
    on the rivers of our blood.

In the miraculous springtime
new leaves open their small green fists
    shake themselves alive in the wind;
    ferns wave their plumes
and the turtles on their leathery feet
    haul themselves out of the mud:
    they shine like new pennies in the sun.
Is this fantasy, myth, the rising
    of the blade of grass, of the fluted stem
    of the early daffodil?
Why then is it so hard to believe
    that one Man long ago in another country
    flowed outward, rose from his grave
the first to cut a path of light
    through the stony density of death?

Even the Stones Sing

Sometimes we wonder how to believe
       when doubt, with iron hands
       grips our throat.
All around us, continuity:
       frivolous leaves dressing the trees
birds with tiny indestructible feet
       hopping about, pecking seed
and the air buzzing
       with tremulous particles of light.

Easy, smoothed over
       pebbles removed
the yellow brick road ribbons
       toward home.
We do not want interferences
       omens in the stars and in the wind
messages in unfolding scrolls
       held at eye level by invisible hosts.
We hold on to what is near:
       table, chair, pen and paper
       trusting the sameness of matter.

How could anyone disbelieve
       the subtle shades of grass
the biography of the crow
       written in black against the sky?
Easy to be linked to the lilac
       even to dust-motes and raindrops
but who can name
       what never appears in the mirror
       next to our face
what never makes a sound
       yet speaks a language of hidden signs?

Sometimes, doubt shakes us
  and we go limp, rag dolls
   slumped on the ground of our being.
We go about our lives
  dumb, blind, scared
until we begin to hear the stones
  in their sealed silence
   singing.

Still Life With Angel

(After a Flemish painting)

On the table, a casual display:
      bowls and dishes, some empty
      others filled with fruit
— glossy apples, grapes in dark clusters —
      round shapes, all, curves
      turning upon themselves to define
      a life held still by habit and use.

On the wall, a convex mirror repeats
      word for word the text of the room.
In the silvered watery glass
      a figure stands, white-robed
      luminous in the outline of bright wings.
— Each pennant burns with rainbow colors —

He does not move: the Seraph
      holds a finger to his smiling lips
      asking nothing but silence and wonder.

Time Does Not Fly:
It Drops

Time, a grey stone
    rubbed smooth by long use
drops with high velocity
    to the vanishing point
    under the heart
    in the bone.
December. We lie as always
    between light and dark
ignoring the boundaries of the flesh
    insisting on knowledge, on love.

Winter in immaculate wraps
    walks the length of the land
    trailing dreams of bears and foxes.
Angels of snow fall slowly
    settling on the hard ground
    the bright folds of their wings.
Pendants of ice chime in the trees
    as the hours drop one by one
    small pebbles in the great void.
The wind speaks a barbaric tongue
    guttural sentences
    announcing ravage and plunder.

Are we going anywhere?
    To the frozen blossoms
    the orbs of crystal in the garden
or down, down, below visibility
    where time breaks open
breaks itself
    against the body of God?

After the Drought

"If you are a poet, you will see clearly that there is a cloud floating in this sheet of paper." (Thich Nhat Hanh, *"Peace Is Every Step"*)

*T*here is a cloud on the page
     a black dot at the left corner.
You can see it through the sentences
     entwined with withered vines
through the words twisted round
     with dark thorns.

After the long drought
     dust powders the land
blurs our story of waiting
     at the mouth of emptiness.

But there is a cloud on the paper:
     it holds a cupful of water.
When tilted, it will spill
     drop by drop, vowels, consonants, verbs.
There will begin to compose note by note
     a cantata involving everything:
stones, leaves, stars and the spirit of God
     singing forth the coming rain.

My Mother, (†MARCH 16, 1983)

She could tell
        the story of my birth
how the cold February sun
        entered the room
        touched the bedstead
        illuminated the scene;
she who was very old
        has been translated by death
into a holy text, a melody
        sung elsewhere by clear gentle voices.
What is left: a blue dress
        a pair of worn shoes
shapes that last summer
        held living flesh
        a body without scars.
She is gone
        and no one now can tell
of that first day, that first sound
        — the modulation sustained in her heart
            through many years, many places.

Her time is now empty
        a rinsed glass
        transparent to the light.

Our Life Spelled Out Clean and Clear

*R*emoteness, absence:
>   the words turn in the mind
like a prayer-wheel
>   circling the dark hub
the presumed emptiness.
Pressing on, our vision tunnels
>   through the night's density
meeting only darkness
>   within darkness.

In the shadows
>   leaves whisper their monotone
and flowers, now colorless
>   bend their frilly heads to the ground.

In the morning, glancing in the mirror
>   we see the contours of our face
an image for a moment frozen flat
>   in the cold diamond of the glass.
Who are we? Are we alone
>   mere specks in galactic space
rappeling down towards death
>   the soul muted and blind?

All time long
>   from the alpha of the first light
>   to the omega of the sun's last ember
God explains himself:
>   he utters a single Word
container of all meaning
>   plainsong from which life is born:
a bounty of people, animals and plants
>   rising, ebbing, cycle after cycle

opening and closing the clasp
linking them each to each.

In the subtext of this world
    of this fabulous invention
our name, our work, our years
    are spelled out clean and clear
a script never to be erased
    never to be lost.

A Work Completed

I look at the work
      rising out of my muscles and bones
        out of my blood.
   Line upon line
      stone upon stone
  the structure grows, moving upwards
      straining towards a single point
        a summit thin as a needle
           drawn out of itself into the air
              by an invisible magnetic power.
  Within, deep underground
      wrapped mummies of knowledge lie buried
       — each strip of cloth wound tight
          compressed in the silence of crypts
           over dry flesh, over dry words.
 But upstairs, the rooms are sunny
     the windows open to the wind
 and I stretch myself, lift my life
     with its weight of pain and joy
 to reach beyond the last sound
    of the last sentence
      of the last poem
 to enter the completed work
    to say "Amen
      it is done
 I hope it is done well."

Reviews

Catherine de Vinck is an extraordinary poet — sensual, evocative, deeply religious. She has found time not to promote her reputation, but simply to write her poems, which spring from genuine love of simple realities like food, weather and people, and suggests a discipline that has turned them and suffering into a poetry of joy.

Sally Cunneen in "The Critic"

In every poem there is imagery — completely original, glorious imagery that delights the mind and heart, filling one with admiration and stirring within one a response of praise, thanks and appreciation, not only for the Creator of all things, but for the creator of this kind of communication.

Rev. Emeric Lawrence in "Worship"

I shall inscribe this book of poems with a warning: Sip these as you would a rare wine — gulping will leave you giddy.

Mary Sullivan in "The Sign"

In contrast to much of modern poetry which laments the disruption, uncertainty and meaninglessness of the human condition, Catherine de Vinck's poetry echoes with affirmations strong enough to transform reality, to gather the fragments of life into human design, to make meaning. It is love which Catherine de Vinck celebrates throughout her poetry, making it immediate rather than distant, sensual rather than impersonal, letting it affirm the significance of human life.

Grace Farrell Lee in "Cross Currents"

To write poetry which speaks directly of Christian mysteries, a poet needs a three-fold gift. He or she must see the world in the light of Christ, must have the power, through language, to mediate new worlds into being, and must discover a way to make these worlds faithful images of the one, both visible and invisible, made and re-made in Christ. Catherine de Vinck has such a gift.

Rev. Robert Pelton in "Restoration"

Catherine de Vinck has developed a poetic voice which expresses the difficult coexistence of searching for meaning along with a painful (yet grateful) surrender to the gift of life. In her *Book of Uncommon Prayers*, she explores dimensions of life which typically arise in her poetry — questions of identity, of vocation, and of communion with God.

Rev. Paul Philibert, OP in "Spirituality Today"

The author possesses the prerequisite of a poet — she has a flawless ear in handling the rhythms of the language, she uses words freshly and solidly, giving to each its full weight of meaning. Catherine de Vinck has a reverence for words, for life. She loves deeply and believes intensely. She has a rich depth of poetic understanding of the mysteries of being.

Virginia Baker in "The Living Church"

Catherine de Vinck's eloquent, beautiful, sensual poems convey an underlying hopefulness and often an ecstatic celebration of living.

Denise Levertov in "Commonweal"

Catherine de Vinck's vision — one that seems terribly hard for the rest of us — is of all time and place bound together in a single moment by Christ, held and redeemed through faith and love despite the agonies of history.... This is not sentimental verse of hopeful pieties, but a work whose particular power comes from her gift as a poet who is able to realize her vision in strong and precise language that draws on a remarkable range of references — nature, the Bible, the liturgy, films, domestic life, anthropology.

Michele Murray in "National Catholic Reporter"